Life On Life, Applying the One-Anothers of Scripture

Welcome to Biblical Mentor Training with Word Of Hope Ministries. For further details about the Mentor Training, please visit the following website:

www.biblicalmentor.com

Word Of Hope Ministries is a Biblical Counseling and Biblical Mentor Training ministry on the Central Coast of California. Please contact us through our website if we can serve you in any way. It would be our privilege and joy!

©2012 Word Of Hope Ministries
Ellen Castillo, Certified Biblical Counselor

"For everything that was written in the past was written to teach us, so that through endurance and the encouragement of the Scriptures we might have hope." (Romans 15:4)

Instructions for group leaders, group participants, and individuals taking the course independently:

If you are taking this course with a group led by Word Of Hope Ministries, you will do homework each week in this workbook and come to the group session to discuss that homework and receive live teaching. The online videos re-cap the live teaching sessions, and are available for absentees or for your future review. You will attend an introductory session, and do Lesson One in your workbook the following week. The second session will be a discussion of Lesson One, with additional live teaching. You will then proceed to Lesson Two, and so on.

If you are taking this course with a group led by someone other than Word Of Hope Ministries, you will do your homework each week in this workbook and view the video teaching sessions either individually as homework or during your session, whichever your group prefers. When you meet with your group, you will discuss the content of both the homework and the video teachings. You will attend an introductory session and then do homework Lesson One in your workbook. You will also view the corresponding video. The second session will be a discussion of Lesson One homework and video. You will then proceed to Lesson Two, and so on.

If you are taking this course individually, complete the homework for each lesson and then view the corresponding video. Feel free to contact Word Of Hope Ministries through our website if you need any assistance. Begin by viewing the introduction video first and reading through the Introduction in the workbook. Then proceed to Lesson One in the workbook, followed by viewing the Lesson One video, and so on.

The following website will take you to the Word Of Hope Mentor Training website. Click on the page on the sidebar that says "Training Course Videos."

www.biblicalmentor.com

*Please note that the <u>workbook does not stand alone</u> — it is incomplete without the videos or live teaching!

*The <u>videos do not stand alone</u> — they are incomplete without the workbook and completed homework!

FOR GROUP LEADERS other than Word Of Hope:

*We suggest that you allow two hours for your sessions, with a break half way through. You are free to use any format you wish, but we do have some suggestions as noted below:

*Open with a welcome and prayer.

*Discuss the prior week's homework from the workbook.

*Discuss the video teachings if you viewed them individually or view them together as a group first and then discuss them.

*You can break up in to smaller groups if needed, and discuss portions of the homework in small groups. You can discuss other portions as a larger group. It is up to you how you handle this, but smaller groups lend themselves to more transparency and sharing.

*Do not go through every bit of the homework page by page, but instead pull out key concepts for discussion. You are free to come up with your own questions to ask the group as well. The goal is not to cover every piece of the workbook, but to be sure your participants are connecting with the main concepts.

If you need help or have questions, don't hesitate to contact us through the contact form on the website homepage.

God bless you as you serve your group! We are in prayer for you!

Table of Contents:

Introduction		9
Lesson One:	Life On Life and the Gospel	29
	A Word of Hope About Your Heart	39
	Applying John 13:34: Love and Devotion	47
	Biblical Mentors: Jesus and His Disciples	53
Lesson Two:	Life On Life, Rooted in God's Word	61
	A Word of Hope About Anger and Forgiveness	69
	Applying Ephesians 4:32: Forgiveness	77
	Biblical Mentors: Paul and Barnabas	81
Lesson Three:	Life On Life In Your Family	87
	A Word of Hope About Worry, Fear, Anxiety and Stress	93
	Applying 1 Thessalonians 4:18: Comfort	99
	Biblical Mentors: Paul and Timothy	103
Lesson Four:	Life On Life in a Culture of Soulcare in the Local Church	109
	A Word of Hope About Depression	117
	Applying Galatians 5:13: Servanthood	125
	Biblical Mentors: Naomi and Ruth	129
Lesson Five:	Life On Life: Prayer	135
	A Word of Hope About Grief and Loss	141
	Applying James 5:16: Prayer	147
	Biblical Mentors: Elijah and Elisha	151
Lesson Six:	Life On Life in Friendship	157
	A Word of Hope About Peacemaking	163
	Applying Hebrews 10:25: Fellowship	169
	Biblical Mentors: Moses and Joshua	173
Lesson Seven:	Life On Life in the Context of Women's Ministry	179
	A Word of Hope About Fear of Man and Insecurity	185
	Applying Romans 15:7: Acceptance	197
	Biblical Mentors: Esther and Mordecai	201

Lesson Eight:	Life On Life in the Context of Student Ministry	207
	A Word of Hope About Decision Making and God's Will	213
	Applying 1 Peter 4:9: Hospitality	221
	Biblical Mentors: Elizabeth and Mary	225
Lesson Nine:	Life On Life Ministry with Difficult People	231
	A Word of Hope about the Thought Life	239
	Applying Ephesians 4:2: Patience and Forbearance	247
	Biblical Mentors: Paul and Titus	251
Lesson Ten:	Life On Life Even While Wounded	257
	A Word of Hope About How People Change	263
	Applying Galatians 6:2: Bearing Burdens	271
	Biblical Mentors: Daniel and Nebuchadnezzar	275
Lesson Eleven:	Life On Life: Boundaries	281
	A Word of Hope About Strongholds	289
	Applying 1 Thessalonians 5:11: Encouragement	297
	Biblical Mentors: Samuel and Saul	301
Lesson Twelve:	Life On Life in YOUR Life	307
	A Word of Hope About Guilt and Regret	315
	Applying Colossians 3:16: Admonishment	325
	Biblical Mentors: Paul an Silas	329
APPENDIX:	One-Another Phrases	335
	Questions to Ask	336
	Heart Diagram	338
	Priorities Diagram	338
	Gospel Diagram	339
	Victory Diagram	339
	Level Two Training Opportunity and Mentor Support	340
	Word Of Hope Ministries Websites	340

All Scripture references are quoted from the New International Version 1984, unless otherwise noted.

©2012 Word Of Hope Ministries

Introduction

Romans 15:4
"For everything that was written in the past was written to teach us, so that through the endurance taught in the Scriptures and the encouragement they provide we might have hope".

LIFE ON LIFE, APPLYING THE ONE-ANTHERS OF SCRIPTURE: INTRODUCTION

Welcome to Life On Life, Applying the One-Anothers of Scripture!

I am so excited that you have decided to take this study. It is the result of many months of seeking God's will and plan for my counseling ministry, "Word Of Hope Ministries." The Lord has led me to spend a portion of my ministry equipping women to minister to other women and girls. Word Of Hope Ministries offers a formal "Biblical Mentor Training" program, which begins with this Bible study as Level One of the training.

As I have spent many hours counseling women and girls, the majority of them Christians, I have observed that many of them would benefit from having someone to walk alongside them, support them, and help them to grow spiritually while dealing biblically with life's circumstances. There is an appropriate time for some to engage in a formal counseling relationship with a trained and experienced Biblical Counselor; I remain committed to providing that opportunity. However, there is also a great need for women and girls to have more natural, less formal relationships with others who are able to apply the One-Anothers of Scripture to their lives. I am aware that the one thing that seems to hinder this kind of informal One-Another ministry is that women feel ill-equipped to be helpers, mentors, disciplers, etc. It is my desire that more women would step into these roles in the lives of those women and girls that God has placed in their spheres of influence. My hope is that this study will give you clarity about your own One-Another ministry.

As this training program developed, it became evident that Level One of the training should have a broader reach in the form of a unique type of Bible course for women that would benefit all women, not just those who want to be trained mentors. So whether you are taking this course simply as a women's Bible study (either in a group or independently) or as a mentor trainee, the goal is that you would gain some tools, knowledge, and insights into what your role is in the lives of others. We will meet this goal by studying several One-Another verses and passages in Scripture, looking at people in the Bible who exemplify excellent One-Another ministry, how to do One-Another ministry in our own lives, and how to offer hope to others from God's Word.

***Romans 15:4** "For everything that was written in the past was written to teach us, so that through the endurance taught in the Scriptures and the encouragement they provide we might have hope".*

All believers are called to engage in some form of One-Another ministry. What is "One-

Another" ministry? It is simply doing life together with other believers, "Life On Life," whether in formal ministry or in the context of your relationships. It is walking alongside someone while reflecting Christ to them as you engage in relationship. Some synonyms for One-Another ministry could be:

*Friendship
*Discipleship
*Mentoring
*Spiritual Friendship
*Counseling
*Soulcare
*Spouse
*Parent
*Serving
*Helping
*Youth Leader
*Women's Ministry Leader
*Sunday School Teacher

Perhaps you see yourself in that list somewhere. If so, then you are in the right study! I hope you are ready to commit to the process and hang in there with it to the end so that you can be well equipped to do excellent One-Another ministry in your own life.

I am committed to praying for you as you go on this new journey with me as you explore God's will for your role in the lives of others. May God richly bless you for honoring Him as you study. May He be glorified!

Privileged to serve you,
Ellen

Bible Study Format:

This study will have a variety of assignments to complete during the week. It is designed for some independent study, which can be done as detailed and as deeply as you desire to take it. You will have a guideline to follow for a study method, but that is flexible and mainly designed to encourage you to be a student of the Word without a structured workbook. This may seem strange and different for you, but it is good for you and can potentially change how you interact with God's Word on a daily basis. This may not seem like your "average" women's Bible study, so I encourage you to hang in there with the process, let go of any preconceived ideas or preferences, and you will see how it all comes together to give you a variety of insights and skills for your personal One-Another relationships.

The Bible study consists of 13 weeks of sessions. You will do some homework over a week's time. You can determine how you accomplish this, but please don't attempt to do it all in one sitting! You will notice that there are additional pages for you to use as you need them or if you wish to take notes on that particular concept during our group sessions, where we will share our insights and findings with one another.

The following is a summary of the four different concepts you will have in each week's homework:

1. Life On Life…is a practical teaching about how to do One-Another ministry in your own sphere of influence. You will have some scriptural and practical questions to consider.

2. A Word of Hope About…is a teaching about how to offer hope from God's Word to women and girls who have a particular common struggle. You will have a case study to work through.

3. Applying…is a study of a One-Another Scripture verse and passage. You will use the Mentor's Bible study Method* for independent study.

4. Biblical Mentors…is an example of discipling/mentoring relationships in Scripture. You will use the Mentor's Bible study Method* for independent study.

*The Mentor's Bible study Method Guide is explained after this introduction.

You can contact Word Of Hope Ministries (Ellen Castillo, Certified Biblical Counselor) at: www.wordofhopeministries.com

You can read more about becoming a Word Of Hope Biblical Mentor through the training program at: www.biblicalmentor.com

Mentor's Bible Study Method:

This is a great method for personal Bible study that would also be very appropriate to use if you are mentoring/discipling another woman or girl. You will become very familiar with it during this study, because it is what you will be using for your homework as you study Biblical Mentors and One-Another sections of each lesson.

As you are doing your personal study in God's Word, it can be helpful to use a "guide." There are many out there, but this one is specifically intended for your use as you go through the Life On Life Bible Study. It is also a method you can use to teach others - maybe someone you are discipling or mentoring yourself, or maybe as a teacher or homeschool mom. Feel free to use it as it is intended - as a GUIDE. That means you can skip the things that don't apply to a particular verse or passage, or add in things that you want to as you decide to dig deeper than this guide takes you. It is up to you how you use it, and it is meant to encourage you to think about God's Word in light of One-Another ministry, how you will apply it to your own life, and specifically how you will apply it as you love others that God puts in your path.

The Mentor's Bible Study Method is something you will become very familiar with. It is, simply, this:

* Meditate
* Memorize
* Meaning
* Meet
* Master
* Mentor

The following Mentor's Bible Study Method Guide is what you will refer to each week as you complete portions of your homework.

Life On Life, Applying the One-Anothers of Scripture

Mentor's Bible Study Method Guide

*Meditate *Memorize *Meaning *Meet *Master *Mentor*

Meditate:
*Pray for understanding and guidance as you seek God's wisdom.
*Read the passage several times, at least 4-5 times. Feel free to read it in several versions and listen to an audio version if you wish.
*Take all or a portion of it, and rewrite it in to your own words (paraphrase).

Memorize:
Read the key verse(s) repeatedly, daily, and commit the key verse(s) to memory.

Meaning:
Some questions to ask about the passage:

* What is the main lesson and what are the overriding spiritual principles in the passage?
* How does this passage pertain to the concept of One-Another ministry specifically?
* Who are the main characters, and what role do they play in the passage?
* What verse(s) are significant in the passage?
* Is there an example to follow?
* Is there an error to avoid?
* Is there something revealed that a person should obey?
* Is there a promise to claim?
* Is there a prayer to echo?
* What cross-references have you discovered that pertain to this study?
* What key words do you see in the passage? (Do a simple word search using a dictionary, concordance, and other Mentor's Resources tools that you wish, for deeper study.)
* If you are studying people in Scripture, do a search on other places this person is mentioned and ask "What insights have I found into this person?" (What is their reputation/character qualities/background/significant events/relationships they were in/personality description, etc.)

This is a guideline, so you can adapt it to the study you are engaged in at the time. Add to it or delete from it so that it is something that works for you.

A note about CONTEXT: As you look to answer some/all of the above questions, remember to always check the context. You do that by reading well before the passage, well after the passage, and by looking at any cross-references you have available. As you look at the context, it is best to read that entire chapter of Scripture or the entire book for deeper context study.

A note about STUDY TOOLS: In order to answer the above questions, be sure to use your Mentor's Resources.

Meet:

Meet with Jesus in the passage! The Bible as a whole is the revelation of Jesus Christ. The Old Testament points to Him, the Gospels give the details of His earthly life, and Acts and Letters show His activity in the world. Therefore, it is possible to find Jesus' presence in all areas of the Bible! From the passage you are studying, find out what you can discover about the nature, ministry, or person of Christ. Look for the Gospel and for discipleship (One-Another) concepts and insights.

Master:

Master the Scripture. Ask yourself "Am I living it?" and plan to be obedient to what you believe the Spirit is saying. Interact with the passage mentally and also on paper to make it personal. You can also briefly write down any further questions you have about what the text means. These questions can be helpful for future study. God can use them to help you understand the Bible better.

Ask yourself "How will I begin to apply what I have learned, how do these insights apply to me personally, and what am I going to do about them?"

Mentor:

After you have studied the passage well, consider again how it ties in to One-Another ministry (such as mentoring, teaching, discipling, etc). Ask the following questions:

* How has this passage challenged me personally?
* How might this passage challenge someone else in my life?
* How can I share hope from this passage?
* Who do I know who needs to have a word of hope right now?

Then, go share the hope! It may not be right now, but after studying a passage with this method, you will have been equipped to share hope with others in your life and ministry. Your insights are not just for you. God has entrusted them to you for His purposes, which includes the purpose of pouring the Truths into others' lives as well.

The above works for topical study, biographical study, and book study. In each lesson's homework, you will find Mentor's Bible Study Method Guide Worksheets for the portions of the lesson on (1) One-Another Scripture application and (2) examples of Biblical mentors.

The workbook will have room for you to write down what you are learning, but you are welcome to add your own notebook paper for more writing, or type it on your computer and then print it out to put in your workbook, if you wish. It is up to you how deep you dig in to the Scriptures. The more you dig, the more you learn and grown.

MENTOR'S RESOURCES:

As you do your lessons, you will want to have several resources that are readily available. It is highly recommended that you use the internet. If you don't have access to a computer at home, you may want to take a trip to the library or a friend's house to do your homework. If you cannot use the internet, perhaps you already own some good study tools that you can use, or borrow them from a library, church library, or friend.

This is not a mandatory list, but just a list of suggestions and study tools that are helpful, either inexpensive or free, and user-friendly. There are, of course, many more "scholarly" tools available as well, if you are one who prefers to do a deeper study of the concepts presented in this study. Typically those will cost you some money, which is noted in these suggestions. It will be up to you how in depth you go in your study each week, but you can definitely do this study without purchasing any additional books. Here is a list of suggested study tools:

Online Bible websites:
*Biblegateway.com   (there is also a good audio Bible here)
*Biblos.com
*Lightsource.com
*Biblica.com
*E-sword.net
*Bible.com
*OnlineBible.net
*Biblia.com
*Biblestudytools.com
*BlueletterBible.org
*Bible.lifeway.com
*esvbible.org
*wbsa.logos.com/Home (this is a topical resource "What the Bible Says About")
There are others, and new ones being added all the time. Do an online search on "online Bible" or "Bible study tools" and see what you can find!

NOTE: Not all online resources are trustworthy. If you are in doubt or have questions about something you find online, please ask a trusted person such as your pastor, or contact Word Of Hope Ministries.

List of sources to use especially for "Word of Hope About" sections of your homework:
Often, Bible study tools will include a topical Bible or topical search option. You can type

in a key word such as "depression" and see what the search brings up. Or, you can use a concordance, and see all the places that word is mentioned in Scripture.

If you cannot find what you need, you can always ask a Biblical Counselor, Pastor, Mentor, or other person you know who may have that knowledge. They just may have a resource to suggest, loan, or point you to.

Refer to a resource book. There are many. The key to this, however, is making sure you are using a reliable, Biblical source. If in doubt, ask someone as in the above suggestion. A series of books worth purchasing if you plan on helping people, is the "Quick Scripture Reference" guides by Patricia A. Miller or John G. Kruis. Another excellent book is "Find it Fast In the Bible" by Ron Rhodes.

As you proceed in this study, you will be pointed to other resources that apply to your current topic. You will also glean from others in the group discussions each week, so don't worry if you don't readily find everything you think you need.

Some items you may want to purchase over time, for your own bookshelf/e-reader/Bible software:

Bible Software such as QuickVerse or Logos (there are many others, too, in varying price ranges)

One Volume Commentaries - a great one that is affordable is "Believer's Bible Commentary" by William MacDonald.

Bible Dictionaries and/or Encyclopedias

Concordance such as Strong's, for the version of Bible you prefer

A Study Bible such as Nelson's Study Bible

A Life Application Study Bible

Additional Resources (you are encouraged to list any that you come across in addition to those already listed, for future reference):

Your Ideas and Thoughts About "One-Another Ministry"

As you enter in to this study, what are your thoughts about One-Another ministry? Take a few moments to briefly respond to the following questions, which are designed to point your thinking towards the need for One-Another ministry in the body of Christ.

Whether you discuss this in a group setting, or are doing this individually, these questions are for you to consider throughout the upcoming study.

NOTE: although the term *mentor* is used here, it really could be substituted with any of the other terms we defined earlier.

MENTORING SURVEY:

1. How would you define the term *mentor*? What kinds of feelings, thoughts, opinions does it raise for you?

2. Do you have someone in your life that you consider a mentor? If so, please briefly define your relationship with her.

3. Do you consider yourself a mentor in someone else's life? If so, please briefly define your relationship with her.

4. Do you have a desire to have a mentor yourself? Why or why not?

5. Do you have a desire to be a mentor to someone? Why or why not?

6. Do you generally feel well-equipped to mentor someone?

7. What holds you back from entering in to a mentoring relationship with someone as a mentor?

8. What holds you back from entering in to a mentoring relationship with someone as the mentee (the one being mentored)?

9. What are your greatest insecurities when it comes to helping women or girls with their

spiritual and emotional health?

10. What qualities, gifts, and skills would you look for in a mentor in your own life?

11. What qualities would you look for in a potential mentee (someone you are walking alongside)?

12. What struggles do you have in your own life that you would benefit from having another woman walk through with you?

13. Among the women you know, what do you see as the greatest struggles they face? (Examples: depression/insecurity/spiritual immaturity/etc.)

14. Regarding those struggles, how well do you think you do at helping these women in general?

15. Are you able to help with the Truths from God's Word that apply to their situations? Why or why not?

16. Is it difficult or fairly easy to be transparent with other women? Do you use your own testimony when walking alongside others? Why or why not?

A WORD OF HOPE ABOUT LONELINESS

There is a very important woman or girl in your midst. She is often present, yet seems invisible. She doesn't openly complain. In fact, maybe she rarely ever speaks at all. She goes unnoticed by most, although she tries to fit in somewhere. She has a lot to offer, but she doesn't feel free to speak her opinions and is too uncomfortable to approach people.

She is lonely.

She can be around a lot of people, yet she is still lonely.

She can be working with the public, yet she is still lonely.

She can be a faithful volunteer in your church, yet she is still lonely.

She can be a leader in your church, yet she is still lonely.

She can be a faithful and loyal friend, yet she is still lonely.

Maybe….she is you…or the woman next to you…or the woman you forget to notice at church every week.

Loneliness is common in our churches - too common. Ask the Lord to use this study to open your eyes to the lonely women and girls that are in your spheres of influence. Ask Him to show you who they are, and to help you know how to approach them and do One-Another ministry with them. Ask Him to sharpen your "radar" to detect the person that needs your encouragement, love, support, friendship, or just a kind gesture. Ask Him to help you to die to self, set your desires aside, and then to be His servant and reach out to others.

It is very easy to come to church ready to socialize with your circle of friends, yet ignore others who are lonely. During the weeks of this study, look around as you attend Bible Study or church and as you engage in other activities with other women and girls. Notice them. If you are not sure how One-Another ministry looks in these situations, this study will help you to gain some insight and tools that will equip you to touch the lives of others, especially the lonely.

Here are some examples of people who can sometimes be lonely:

*Singles
*Elderly
*Widowed
*Handicapped
*Popular or talented people
*Affluent people
*Impoverished people
*People of a different culture than ours
*Can you think of others?

God's Word has some things to say to us about loneliness. Look up the following Scriptures, and write down how they speak to the way that we are to minister to the lonely.

*Genesis 2:18

*1 Kings 19:14-18

*Psalm 68:6

*Ecclesiastes 4:10-11

*Matthew 28:20

Although loneliness and being alone can go hand in hand, this isn't necessarily always the case. Some of the time, being alone isn't a negative thing unless it is causing the person to feel an inner emptiness. Loneliness is the most frequently expressed complaint in counseling, both secular and Christian. Loneliness and insecurity often occur simultaneously, and that often bears destructive fruit. A lonely person is tempted to cope with the pain with something — anything — that might bring some relief. If that relief is not found in Christ, the loneliness will continue to be a struggle.

Other than God, list some things that a lonely person might turn to:

How do you offer hope to a person who is suffering with loneliness? As you gain insight and tools to do excellent One-Another ministry in your sphere of influence, you will most certainly come across the lonely woman or girl. What would you say at first to a believer who tells you that they are lonely? What questions might you ask them? What direction would you give them? Jot down some ideas here:

As a follower of Jesus Christ, our model for caring for one another is Jesus Himself. No doubt, He experienced extreme loneliness — He was separated from the Father on the cross. But He also had friends who played a One-Another role in His life as well as He in theirs. In John's account of the last evening Jesus spent with His disciples, Jesus told them, "My command is this: Love each other as I have loved you. Greater love has no one than this, that he lay down his life for his friends. You are my friends if you do what I command. I no longer call you servants, because a servant does not know his master's business. Instead, I have called you friends, for everything that I learned from my Father I have made known to you. You did not choose me, but I chose you and appointed you to go and bear fruit—fruit that will last. Then the Father will give you whatever you ask in my name. This is my command: Love each other." (John 15:12-17)

Jesus' command was to LOVE EACH OTHER. He put no conditions on it. It was not a suggestion. This command is blatantly clear for us in Scripture - we must love each other… not just those who are nice, or just the people we like, or the ones who are the most within our comfort zones, or the ones we understand the best, or the ones that make us feel good about ourselves. That lonely woman or girl may not fit in to any of these requirements that we must admit we all have at times. She may be difficult to approach, or even difficult to love. But what are we commanded to do? Love her.

There are a variety of ways to love. Love is an action, not a feeling. What more loving thing can we do than offer them HOPE. We do that with God's very words from Scripture.

As you help someone who is lonely, you can offer them the following Truths:

*God created man with an inherent need for social relationships (Gen. 2:18). God created man in His own image (Gen. 1:27), and God is a social being (Gen. 1:26). A social relationship exists among the persons of the Trinity — the Father, Son, and Holy Spirit. Without relationship, there will be loneliness. Therefore, the first encouragement a lonely person needs is to start building relationships.

*The most lonely time in history was when the Father deserted the Son and Jesus was left alone as He bore our sins (see Matthew 27:46).

"About the ninth hour Jesus cried out in a loud voice, *"Eloi, Eloi, lama sabachthani?"* — which means, "My God, my God, why have you forsaken me?" (Matthew 27:46)

The lonely person needs to understand that Jesus understands their loneliness, and experienced it Himself.

There are others in the Bible who suffered from loneliness. Take a look at just a few in the following Scriptures.

*Cain due to sin (Gen. 4:13-14)

*Job due to physical ailment (Job 6:15-21)

*Elijah due to self pity (1 Kings 19:1-21) and standing for righteousness (Jer. 20:7-9)

*David due to sin (Psalm 25:16) and due to opposition (Psalm 143:4)

*Paul due to being forsaken by friends (2 Tim. 4:9-11)

2 Timothy 4:9-22 tells us about loneliness and how to deal with it:

"9 Do your best to come to me quickly, 10 for Demas, because he loved this world, has deserted me and has gone to Thessalonica. Crescens has gone to Galatia, and Titus to Dalmatia. 11 Only Luke is with me. Get Mark and bring him with you, because he is helpful to me in my ministry. 12 I sent Tychicus to Ephesus. 13 When you come, bring the cloak that I left with Carpus at Troas, and my scrolls, especially the parchments.

¹⁴ Alexander the metalworker did me a great deal of harm. The Lord will repay him for what he has done. ¹⁵ You too should be on your guard against him, because he strongly opposed our message.

¹⁶ At my first defense, no one came to my support, but everyone deserted me. May it not be held against them. ¹⁷ But the Lord stood at my side and gave me strength, so that through me the message might be fully proclaimed and all the Gentiles might hear it. And I was delivered from the lion's mouth. ¹⁸ The Lord will rescue me from every evil attack and will bring me safely to his heavenly kingdom. To him be glory for ever and ever. Amen."

…Verses 9 and 11 address the need for good companionship. It is important not to isolate ourselves. Paul desired to be among God's people. So should we.

…Verses 17-18 address the need for a close relationship with God. The Savior is the only cure for loneliness. Knowing Him deeply is satisfying to the soul, and even during a season of being alone, loneliness does not need to prevail in a person's heart if she knows God intimately and personally. No amount of socializing can fill the need the way a healthy relationship with Jesus Christ does. A person can know God's presence (vs. 17a), purpose (vs. 17b), and promises (vs 18), through His Word. And God puts us in each other's lives to speak these Truths from God's Word to one another.

These are some basic Truths from God's Word that can encourage and help (thus, love) a lonely person. What other Truths from Scripture come to mind that you could use to encourage and help a lonely person?

Obviously, God would not have put so many One-Another verses in Scripture if we were not meant to minister in a variety of ways to one another! We will look at this topic from a variety of angles over the coming weeks. Pray that we would be vessels for His purposes in the lives of others.

*1 Peter 3:15: "But in your hearts set apart Christ as Lord. **Always** be **prepared** to give an answer to everyone who asks you to give the reason for the hope that you have."*

As you dig in to your weekly lessons, ask The Lord to use them to prepare you to always be ready to share hope!

Lesson One

John 13:34
"A new command I give you: Love one another. As I have loved you, so you must love one another."

LIFE ON LIFE and the Gospel

Why do we need to understand and apply the One-Anothers of Scripture? What is our goal? The goal should be to get the Gospel out to others. The two commandments (love God and others, and go and make disciples) are so closely tied together that one can't work without the other.

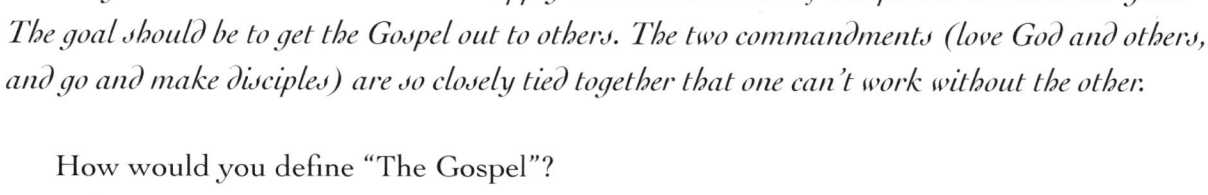

How would you define "The Gospel"?

What are the essentials of a Gospel message?

How could you explain the Gospel to someone who has never heard it?

The Gospel has to be our starting point for all One-Another ministry. The implication in the One-Anothers is that we are to do life with other believers, Life On Life. Of course, we also do life with nonbelievers, but the One-Anothers emphasize the role we play in each other's lives, believer to believer.

If you are in a relationship with a woman or girl that God has placed in your life and she has understood a clear Gospel and is a Christian, you have a very good starting point for One-Another life together. If you are not sure she understands a clear Gospel, you have an opportunity to share it! How often have you asked a new friend (or old one for that matter) what they think the Gospel is and how it applies to their life? We can't miss this! It's not only our starting point for Life On Life, but it is the ending point and everything in the middle, too.

The Gospel is for salvation. It is also to be applied to our lives from that point on. It is not to be applied in the sense that your salvation depends on performing a certain way or upholding a certain standard of perfection. It is to be applied in the sense that you know it, understand it, can explain it, and BELIEVE it. In the process of living life, the Gospel applied has the potential to either gradually or immediately change how you behave, how you relate to people, how you make decisions, how you view people, how you view yourself, and everything else about how you live.

Often women are intimidated about talking about the Gospel. Let's start this study by being honest about this in our own lives and ask God to help us to be able to explain a clear Gospel and to understand it and apply it to our own lives before we can help someone else.

What makes many women so weak in this area? Is it fear? Lack of understanding? Maybe they are not sure they can articulate it clearly. Maybe they are afraid they will say something wrong. Sometimes they are afraid that they won't be able to back up what they say from Scripture, forgetting where to find the verses. There are many reasons that could be added to this list. In a One-Another situation, one of the very best ways you can share the Gospel is to share your own story of salvation. You can talk about what your life was like before you came to know Christ and what was happening when you first came to belief. You can talk about your understanding of the Gospel, and how it transformed you upon salvation and how it continues to transform you now. Sometimes, our own stories speak more clearly than going through a formulated "Gospel presentation."

There is an account in the Bible about a woman that you are probably familiar with and how Jesus shared the Gospel message with her. The story of the woman at the well is found in

John 4:7-26. Please read it in your Bible, then come back here to see what we can glean from this account.

Jesus did not use a "formula" to share the Gospel with the woman. In this passage, we can take note of some ways to share a clear Gospel and to be sure it is understood:

* Jesus met the woman when she was alone. Often, people will be more honest if nobody else is listening.

* Jesus began with her immediate need — not spiritual, but tangible (v. 7). Because she was not a believer, she could not discern spiritual things (1 Cor. 2:14). Therefore, He spoke about something she could relate to — water. We can approach people in the same manner of developing conversation. If we are not certain they are a believer, we can make them more comfortable by starting with tangible conversations.

* Jesus, after establishing tangible conversation, turned to the spiritual (v. 10). He simply talked of the things of God. The questions we ask could help us to see if the person understands what being a Christian means. We could ask "Are you involved in church?" or even "Do you love God?" We could then move on to asking about her salvation testimony and asking what her walk with The Lord is currently like. For us, this can take courage.

* If this conversation reveals that the person does not have a personal relationship with Jesus Christ, then you can follow Jesus' example from this passage before you go any further in relating with her. Verses 16-18 show how Jesus brought conviction, using the Law and gently pointing out her transgression. Gently speak with her and let The Holy Spirit do the convicting; let Him direct you as to what to say. Once she comes to an admission of her guilt, she is ready for hope.

* Jesus then revealed Himself to the woman at the well (v. 26). She was ready for grace. If the person you are talking to is ready for grace, be sure to present the work of the cross — that God sent His Son to suffer and die in our place. Tell her of the love of God in Christ, Jesus' resurrection from the dead, and the defeat of death. You can say something like, "It's as simple as this. We broke God's Law, and Jesus paid our fine. If you repent and trust in the Savior, God forgives your sins and dismisses your case." Be sure to include the essentials we talked about at the beginning of this lesson. If a person is truly broken over her sins and grateful to God, then her confession will flow without prompting, either silently or verbally to you. Be sure to pray with her. Make sure she has a Bible. Encourage her to go to a Bible-believing church. Start a One-Another relationship with her, Life On Life!

Any kind of mentoring, discipling, friendship, and all One-Another ministry should continue to be rooted in the Gospel. One of the best tools for One-Another relationships is this phrase: APPLY THE GOSPEL.

What do you think is meant by "apply the Gospel"?

As you do Life On Life with someone applying the One-Anothers of Scripture with her, you will find that there will be many opportunities to share hope. Women and girls struggle in all kinds of areas. You are likely to bump into some of these struggles if you have any kind of ministry, family life, or social life. Once you are fairly certain that someone has grasped the Gospel for salvation, the help you give her from there is to help her to see the need for and ability to APPLY the Gospel to her life. You want to always be sure that you are not giving her the idea that she needs to change her behavior or mindset in order to earn approval, acceptance, or even worse, salvation. Always emphasize her eternal security; struggling people often struggle to believe this Truth. Remind her of her identity in Christ and how He views her. It is not because she earned it, but because of the Gospel — His finished work on her behalf.

Future lessons will help you to know how to share hope with others; you will want to recall the phrase "APPLY THE GOSPEL." It will direct you in your help towards others, assuring you are always Christ-focused and sticking to Biblical principles.

Don't worry if this concept is not clear or foreign to you. As you study more week by week about doing Life On Life, sharing hope with others, and applying the One-Anothers, it will become your most common "tool" in your conversations.

Let's look at a few phrases you might catch on to as you speak with people that could indicate that they either do not have a clear understanding of the Gospel or that they are not applying it to their lives:

*"I don't understand why God would do this to me."
*"I can't see any purpose in this."
*"I just don't know who I am anymore."
*"I am so anxious and worried all the time."

*"I feel so guilty."
*"I do not deserve another chance."
*"I don't feel forgiven."
*"He hurt me too badly; I can't forgive him."

Let's look at those again, and see how the Gospel might apply. realize that although we don't have the full story in each of these scenarios, this is meant to show you what we mean by "apply the Gospel." You will have opportunities in each week's homework and discussion time to apply the Gospel in some more specific situations. This time, let's look at a Gospel Truth that applies to each (look up these Scriptures as you read these):

*"I don't understand why God would do this to me." — The cross tells us He suffered everything we do as He bore our sins (1 Peter 2:24).

*"I can't see any purpose in this." — The cross is why He can promise to work all things together, because it was the ultimate working together for good on our behalf (John 19:28-30).

*"I just don't know who I am anymore." — At the cross, we find our identity, upon conversion we are a new creation (2 Cor 5:17).

*"I am so anxious and worried all the time." — God made provision for you at the cross in every area, proving Himself completely trustworthy as your Heavenly Father (Philippians 4:6).

*"I still feel so guilty." — You are forgiven at the cross, whether you feel like it or not (1 John 1:9).

*"I do not deserve another chance." — Grace, because of the cross, flows freely (Romans 3:24).

*"I don't feel forgiven." — God's Word says that you are forgiven when you place your faith in Him (Ephesians 1:7).

*"He hurt me too badly, I can't forgive him." — We don't deserve God's forgiveness, either, but we are forgiven (Romans 4:7).

*Others?

<u>Here are more Truths of the Gospel that are applicable to more than just our initial conversion:</u>

*The Gospel binds me eternally to the loving Father.
*The Gospel provides my daily security to wrestle with my own sin.
*The Gospel promises to complete the work of redemption in my life.

*The Gospel shapes my identity as a human being.

*The Gospel makes intimate communication with God possible.

*The Gospel protects me from pride and self-righteousness.

*The Gospel compels me to live mercifully with others.

*The Gospel convicts my heart to war against sin.

*The Gospel makes it possible to war with sin.

*The Gospel portrays the rich, eternal, incomprehensible, overwhelming love of Jesus Christ to me.

*Can you think of others?

As you engage in a One-Another relationship, after you have helped someone to apply the Gospel and she grasps these Truths, you can also apply Scriptural principles, commands, and promises to her situations. Another useful phrase for you to learn and remember is "THINK BIBLICALLY." If a woman does not have a good understanding and application of the gospel, these other principles, commands and promises will not be as useful. Both the Gospel and these other Biblical principles are things that we need to always "think Biblically" about for spiritual health. The Gospel is your starting point, midpoint, and ending point when we all engage in perfect One-Another relationship with Jesus in Heaven! We also must always encourage others to think Biblically and be sure that we, ourselves are doing the same.

As you do Life On Life with others, every relationship should begin with the following Truths that are especially important in One-Another, Life On Life relationships (look up these verses as you read):

*The Good News:

1. God loves us (John 3:16-17).

2. God redeems us (Romans 3:21-31).

3. God makes all things new (2 Corinthians 5:17; Revelation 21:5).

*Eternal Fellowship With Christ:

1. Salvation is a work of Christ, not us (Ephesians 2:9).

2. We are reborn by Him (Ephesians 2:1-7).

3. We are adopted by Him (Romans 8:15-17).

4. We are cleansed by Him (Hebrews 10:22 and 1 John 1:9).

5. We are taught by Him (John 6:45).

6. We are secured by Him (John 6:37-40).
*The Good News Changes Those Who Believe It:
1. Regeneration (2 Corinthians 5:17).
2. Renewal (Romans 12:1-2; 2 Corinthians 4:16).
*The Good News empowers us to obey God's Word.
1. Willingness and ability to obey (Romans 6:1-3; Romans 6:4-7; 2 Corinthians 5:14-17).
2. Willingness and ability to share the Good News with others (2 Corinthians 5:18-21).

Look again at the woman at the well (John 4:28-42). After the woman received the Truth, she immediately went and told others. As a result, many believed. She exemplified One-Another ministry immediately upon belief. She did not wait to learn a formula or a program to start a ministry. She simply went out and shared her story. Let's do the same, as we minister Life On Life according to the One-Anothers of Scripture.

What is your starting point when sharing hope with another woman or girl? Write it again here:

In your next homework section, you will have an opportunity in the form of a case study to apply the Gospel and think biblically as you learn how to share hope from God's Word with someone who is struggling.

Additional Notes, Lesson One: Life On Life and the Gospel

(Use this for extra homework space and to take notes on our session discussion)

A WORD OF HOPE About Your Heart

❧

Remember: APPLY THE Gospel and THINK BIBLICALLY are your key One-Another phrases that you will want to keep in mind as you approach sharing a Word of hope with another.

Before we can share hope with someone, we need to have a better understanding of "the heart." Biblically, what do we mean when we say "the heart"?
The heart is everything immaterial about you. It is your thoughts, beliefs, and desires at the core. From that core flow your motives, behaviors, attitudes, and emotions — the things that make up your personality.

In order to have lasting change that is rooted in the Truth of Scripture (the Gospel and thinking Biblically), there needs to be true "heart change." Ephesians 4:20-24 addresses how change happens. We will be covering this more in depth in a future lesson.

All Biblical help, regardless what you call it, must begin with the Gospel and how it applies to the heart. Defining the heart is critical. The diagram you will find on the next page is a helpful tool to explain it more clearly.

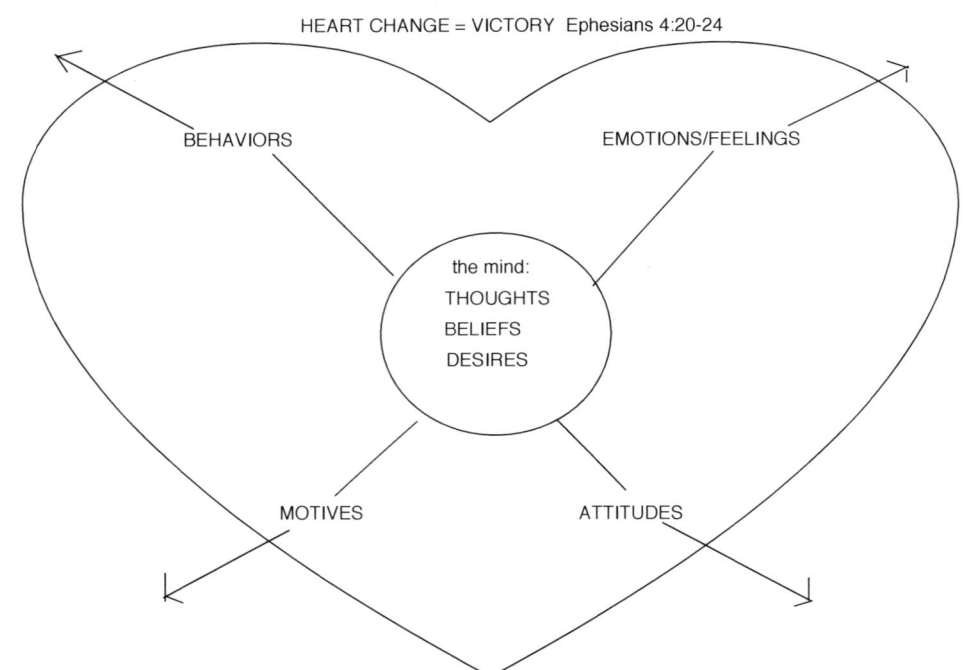

```
                    HEART CHANGE = VICTORY  Ephesians 4:20-24

              BEHAVIORS                    EMOTIONS/FEELINGS


                            the mind:
                            THOUGHTS
                            BELIEFS
                            DESIRES


              MOTIVES                      ATTITUDES
```

Gospel driven thoughts, beliefs, and desires occur in our minds. They are revealed in our motives, attitudes, behaviors, and emotions, which will flow out of our hearts. Heart change must start by applying the gospel to your thoughts, beliefs, and desires. This will lead to change in your behaviors, emotions, motives, and attitudes. 2 Corinthians 5:17.

So, you can see above that all change must begin in the core of the heart. Everything else pours out of our thoughts, beliefs, and desires. If our thoughts, beliefs, and desires are not Gospel-centered, our attitudes, motives, emotions, and behaviors will not be godly.

God's Word says that we cannot trust our own hearts. Jeremiah 17:9 says, "The heart is deceitful above all things and beyond cure. Who can understand it?" This is why we cannot help someone by simply offering a new behavior modification idea, or telling them how they should or shouldn't be feeling, or what their motives should be or that they need to change their attitude. Those things can be changed in our own strength for a short period of time, but there will be no lasting change until we get to the core — our thoughts, beliefs, and desires.

Our thoughts are how we spend our thought life. Are our thoughts centered on this "checklist" of sorts found in Philippians 4:8?

"Finally, brothers, whatever is true, whatever is noble, whatever is right, whatever is pure, whatever is lovely, whatever is admirable—if anything is excellent or praiseworthy—think about such things." (Philippians 4:8)

Or are we thinking thoughts that deny God's sovereignty, or deny the Truths of the Gospel and are full of the fleshly worries, fears, and anxieties?

Our beliefs are what we believe about God and His Word. Our theology and doctrine matter. If we are in error, our beliefs will eventually pour in to our attitudes or behaviors, emotions and motives. Again, we must be rooted in the Gospel and we must think Biblically.

Our desires are simply what we want. Do we want God's will or our own? Do we want self-centered things in life, or do we want to be others-centered? Is there idolatry in our lives, or are we applying Ephesians 4:22-24?

"You were taught, with regard to your former way of life, to put off your old self, which is being corrupted by its deceitful desires; to be made new in the attitude of your minds; and to put on the new self, created to be like God in true righteousness and holiness."

As you engage in Life On Life relationships, keep in mind to always encourage others that it is God Who does a work in their hearts, and it is not just about changing their external lifestyles. God is a relational God, and Jesus is our perfect example of how to care for others. His work in your life was and is a work at the heart level. He never says to "clean up your act" and then come to Him. Instead, He gave and continues to give you grace, patiently working in your heart as you grow in love, knowledge, and application of His Word in your life. You must now do the same as you relate to others — focus on the heart need, helping them to apply the Gospel and to think Biblically, and don't focus primarily on the externals. Be patient, and practice the One-Anothers of Scripture in your relationships. Remember that it is God Who will work in their hearts.

It is always good to ask God to search your heart and do some self-examination!

The following are some things that will give you more fruitful One-Another ministry and could be considered "qualifications" of someone who mentors, teaches, disciples, etc.

Look through them, and note which areas are strengths and which areas are weaknesses.

*Be more of a listener than answer-giver.
*Be certain that you, as a believer, are called to it.
*Esteem others more highly than yourself.
*Love God with all your heart, soul, mind and strength.
*Have a strong love for God's people of all ages.
*Have a love for God's Word.
*Know how to go to God's Word for answers, rather than secular sources.
*Enjoy seeing people transformed by God's Word.
*Be willing to be stretched beyond your comfort zone.
*Be willing to let God work in your heart, starting with your thoughts, beliefs, and desires.

*Be willing to be committed, even when people are difficult.

*Be willing to seek counsel for yourself when you are struggling.

*Be humble, patient, and kind towards others.

*Have regular devotional time and Bible Study for your own walk.

*Have a meaty prayer life.

*Memorize Scripture.

*Serve the body in your local church.

*Attend church regularly.

*Fellowship with believers regularly.

*Evangelize in your sphere of influence.

*Read quality books from Christian authors that challenge you to grow.

*Listen to theologically and doctrinally sound Christian music as a worship tool.

*Teach and mentor others to do all the above.

Commit now to working on the areas of weakness you noted above. Write a prayer here, between you and The Lord, asking for His guidance in your life as you engage in One-Another, Life On Life ministry with others He places in your path.

✝ A Word of Hope about Your Heart, CASE STUDY:

We will have a case study in this section of your homework each week, taking a look at how to share hope with somebody with a particular struggle. This week, we will look at a woman who is feeling hopeless about her life. Susan has gone through many trials lately, none of them in her control. Her husband lost his job due to the bad economy, and they are in danger of foreclosing on their home that they have enjoyed for 15 years. They have 3 grown children, all living in other states. Their oldest daughter just found out that she is infertile, and Susan has always longed for grandchildren. Susan's best friend recently got diagnosed with breast cancer, and Susan struggles to know how to be a friend to her when Susan herself is feeling so hopeless. Due to their financial troubles, they also have been unable to meet their monthly bills, and she and her husband have no idea how to remedy that. Susan does not work, and has always been a stay at home wife and mom. In addition to all of that, Susan's car needs repairs, her washing machine is making a loud noise, her computer crashed, and she feels as if things are literally falling apart around her. Susan has been a Christian, she says, since she was 15. She received Christ while at a Christian camp one summer, and started attending a Bible believing church at that time. She and her husband go to a solid church on a regular basis, and she serves as a volunteer in the nursery. She attends Women's Bible Studies on occasion. She has a few friends in the church, but nobody she considers herself close to. She feels terrible about saying this, but she feels like God has abandoned her. She even feels a bit angry with Him for allowing all of these struggles at the same time, with no visible solution in sight. She is not sleeping well, due to the anxiety and worry all of this is causing. She is very close to asking her doctor for an anti-anxiety drug to help her to feel better.

    You go to church with Susan, and you end up sitting next to her at an event with plenty of time to chat. She tells you her story with all of the above details. How would you encourage Susan in that moment? How could you encourage her over time after that conversation?

Additional Notes, Lesson One: A Word of Hope About Your Heart

(Use this for extra homework space and to take notes on our session discussion)

APPLYING JOHN 13:34: Love and Devotion

John 13:34

"A new command I give you: Love one another. As I have loved you, so you must love one another."

You will study this most accurately by reading in context John 13:31-38, which is the broader passage that this verse is taken from. Remember that our focus for this study is One-Another ministry, so you will want to study that and related themes as you dig in.

For your study of this week's One-Another Scripture, use the Mentor's Bible Study Method Guide below. If you are doing this study in a group, we will have a discussion in the next session about your study findings and how it applies to the concept of One-Another ministry. Don't be intimidated or afraid to dig deep! Don't worry if you come up with more questions than answers — that's a part of in-depth Bible Study. It's ok! Just learn what you can by giving it your best effort. This kind of independent Bible study is stretching for us and good for us. Enjoy the process!

Mentor's Bible Study Method Guide

*Meditate *Memorize *Meaning *Meet *Master *Mentor*

Meditate:
*Pray for understanding and guidance as you seek God's wisdom.
*Read the passage several times, at least 4-5. Feel free to read it in several versions and listen to an audio version if you wish.
*Take all or a portion of it, and rewrite it in to your own words (paraphrase).

Memorize:
Read the key verse(s) repeatedly, daily, and commit the key verse(s) to memory.

Meaning:
Some questions to ask about the passage:

* What is the main lesson and what are the overriding spiritual principles in the passage?
* How does this passage pertain to the concept of One-Another ministry specifically?
* Who are the main characters, and what role do they play in the passage?
* What verse(s) are significant in the passage?
* Is there an example to follow?
* Is there an error to avoid?
* Is there something revealed that a person should obey?
* Is there a promise to claim?
* Is there a prayer to echo?
* What cross-references have you discovered that pertain to this study?
* What key words do you see in the passage? (Do a simple word search using a dictionary, concordance, and other Mentor's Resources tools that you wish, for deeper study.)
* If you are studying people in Scripture, do a search on other places this person is mentioned and ask "what insights have I found into this person?" (What is their reputation/character qualities/background/significant events/relationships they were in/personality description, etc.)

This is a guideline, so you can adapt it to the study you are engaged in at the time. Add to it or delete from it so that it is something that works for you.

A note about CONTEXT: As you look to answer some/all of the above questions, remember to always check the context. You do that by reading well before the passage, well after the passage, and by looking at any cross-references you have available. As you look at the context, it is best to read that entire chapter of Scripture or the entire book for deeper context study.

A note about STUDY TOOLS: In order to answer the above questions, be sure to use your Mentor's Resources.

Meet:
Meet with Jesus in the passage! The Bible as a whole is the revelation of Jesus Christ. The Old Testament points to Him, the Gospels give the details of His earthly life, and Acts and Letters show His activity in the world. Therefore, it is possible to find Jesus' presence in all areas of the Bible! From the passage you are studying, find out what you can discover about the nature, ministry, or person of Christ. Look for the Gospel and for discipleship (One-Another) concepts and insights.

<u>Master</u>:
*Master the Scripture. Ask yourself, "Am I living it?" and plan to be obedient to what you believe the Spirit is saying. Interact with the passage mentally and also on paper to make it personal. You can also briefly write down any further questions you have about what the text means. These questions can be helpful for future study. God can use them to help you understand the Bible better.

*Ask yourself, "How will I begin to apply what I have learned, how do these insights apply to me personally, and what am I going to do about them?"

<u>Mentor</u>:
After you have studied the passage well, consider again how it ties in to One-Another ministry (such as mentoring, teaching, discipling, etc). Ask the following questions:

* How has this passage challenged me personally?

* How might this passage challenge someone else in my life?
* How can I share hope from this passage?
* Who do I know who needs to have a word of hope right now?

Then, go share the hope! It may not be right now, but after studying a passage with this method, you will have been equipped to share hope with others in your life and ministry. Your insights are not just for you. God has entrusted them to you for His purposes, which includes the purpose of pouring the Truths into others' lives as well.

BIBLICAL MENTORS: Jesus and His Disciples

John 15:12-17

¹² My command is this: Love each other as I have loved you. ¹³ Greater love has no one than this: to lay down one's life for one's friends. ¹⁴ You are my friends if you do what I command. ¹⁵ I no longer call you servants, because a servant does not know his master's business. Instead, I have called you friends, for everything that I learned from my Father I have made known to you. ¹⁶ You did not choose me, but I chose you and appointed you so that you might go and bear fruit—fruit that will last—and so that whatever you ask in my name the Father will give you. ¹⁷ This is my command: Love each other.

You will study this passage most accurately by reading it in context in the whole chapter of John 15.

This passage portrays the example of Jesus' One-Another ministry to His disciples. Study this week's passage, but feel free to expand on that as God leads you. There are other places in Scripture that elaborate on this particular relationship beyond this passage.

For your study of this week's example of Biblical mentors, use the Mentor's Bible Study Method Guide below. If you are doing this study in a group, we will have a discussion in the next session about your study findings and how it applies to the concept of One-Another ministry. Don't be intimidated or afraid to dig deep! Don't worry if you come up with more questions than answers - that's a part of in depth Bible Study and it's ok. Just learn what you can by giving it your best effort. This kind of independent Bible study is stretching for us, and good for us. Enjoy the process!

Mentor's Bible Study Method Guide

*Meditate *Memorize *Meaning *Meet *Master *Mentor*

<u>Meditate:</u>
*Pray for understanding and guidance as you seek God's wisdom.
*Read the passage several times, at least 4-5. Feel free to read it in several versions and listen to an audio version if you wish.
*Take all or a portion of it, and rewrite it in to your own words (paraphrase).

<u>Memorize:</u>
Read the key verse(s) repeatedly, daily, and commit the key verse(s) to memory.

<u>Meaning:</u>
Some questions to ask about the passage:

* What is the main lesson and what are the overriding spiritual principles in the passage?
* How does this passage pertain to the concept of One-Another ministry specifically?
* Who are the main characters, and what role do they play in the passage?
* What verse(s) are significant in the passage?
* Is there an example to follow?
* Is there an error to avoid?
* Is there something revealed that a person should obey?
* Is there a promise to claim?
* Is there a prayer to echo?
* What cross-references have you discovered that pertain to this study?
* What key words do you see in the passage? (Do a simple word search using a dictionary, concordance, and other Mentor's Resources tools that you wish, for deeper study.)

* If you are studying people in Scripture, do a search on other places this person is mentioned and ask "what insights have I found into this person?" (What is their reputation/character qualities/background/significant events/relationships they were in/personality description, etc.)

This is a guideline, so you can adapt it to the study you are engaged in at the time. Add to it or delete from it so that it is something that works for you.

A note about CONTEXT: As you look to answer some/all of the above questions, remember to always check the context. You do that by reading well before the passage, well after the passage, and by looking at any cross-references you have available. As you look at the context, it is best to read that entire chapter of Scripture or the entire book for deeper context study.

A note about STUDY TOOLS: In order to answer the above questions, be sure to use your Mentor's Resources.

Meet:
Meet with Jesus in the passage! The Bible as a whole is the revelation of Jesus Christ. The Old Testament points to Him, the Gospels give the details of His earthly life, and Acts and Letters show His activity in the world. Therefore, it is possible to find Jesus' presence in all areas of the Bible! From the passage you are studying, find out what you can discover about the nature, ministry, or person of Christ. Look for the Gospel and for discipleship (One-Another) concepts and insights.

Master:
*Master the Scripture. Ask yourself "Am I living it?" and plan to be obedient to what you believe the Spirit is saying. Interact with the passage mentally and also on paper to make it personal. You can also briefly write down any further questions you have about what the text means. These questions can be helpful for future study. God can use them to help you understand the Bible better.

*Ask yourself "How will I begin to apply what I have learned, how do these insights apply to me personally, and what am I going to do about them?"

Mentor:
After you have studied the passage well, consider again how it ties in to One-Another ministry (such as mentoring, teaching, discipling, etc). Ask the following questions:

* How has this passage challenged me personally?
* How might this passage challenge someone else in my life?
* How can I share hope from this passage?
* Who do I know who needs to have a word of hope right now?

Then, go share the hope! It may not be right now, but after studying a passage with this method, you will have been equipped to share hope with others in your life and ministry. Your insights are not just for you. God has entrusted them to you for His purposes, which includes the purpose of pouring the Truths into others' lives as well.

Lesson Two

Ephesians 4:32
"Be kind and compassionate to one another, forgiving each other, just as in Christ God forgave you."

LIFE ON LIFE, Rooted in God's Word

Theology and doctrine matter a great deal in Life On Life, One-Another relationships. Theology (what you believe about God) and doctrine (what you believe about God's Word) will influence your heart in every area — thoughts, beliefs, and desires which pour out in to motives, attitudes, emotions, and behaviors. (Refer back to the diagram in Lesson One.)

Here are some thought provoking statements for you to consider that determine what you believe about God and His Word. Mark T or F next to them. Then, see if you can find a Scripture or two to back up what you believe about that statement if it is true, or to contradict it if it is false. Make a note of the Scripture reference next to the sentence. You can use any tools to find the Scriptures that you wish. An online source or a reference book would be helpful. You can even do an online search. If you are unable to find verses, don't worry; we are going to cover this in our next session together. Give it a try!

1. Jesus Christ is the only means of salvation.

2. There are things that are true for all people, in all places, at all times.

3. Our good works play no part in our salvation.

4. Apart from Christ, people are bad at their core.

5. God is in control of everything at all times.

6. The future is planned by God.

7. The Devil is completely under God's authority.

8. Salvation is the work of God, not man.

9. Nothing occurs that is not ordained by God.

10. Only those who put their faith in Christ go to Heaven.

11. No one deserves to be saved.

12. God's purposes are never thwarted.

13. Truth is not relative.

14. God personally spoke the world into existence.

15. Self (the flesh) is a person's worst enemy.

16. The Bible is divinely written by God through man.

17. The Bible is pertinent to all people at all times and is not bound by time (not outdated).

God's Word and our hearts are entirely connected. The Bible is very realistic about human suffering of all kinds. It is also descriptive about what motivates us and drives us in our relationships. Woven through stories, we find God's promises to redeem our suffering and transform our hearts. We are exposed as victims and victimizers, sufferers and sinners. With a Biblical view of God, self, and suffering, we are empowered by His Spirit to own up to our faults, forgive those who sin against us, and trust God while we move forward with renewed thoughts, beliefs, and desires.

Without this core belief about Scripture as our basis for relationships, we cannot possibly engage in healthy, fruitful One-Another lifestyles. Apart from God's Word, we have no basis for helping others, caring for others, or relating to others. All that would be left is our flesh; whenever flesh rules in a relationship, there is struggle.

We live in a day and age where even believers have not trusted in the sufficiency of God's Word to have the answers they need to life's dilemmas, struggles, problems, and worries. We are too often prone to refer someone to a secular source of help than we are to point them to what God's Word has to offer.

If a woman comes to you and says, "I am feeling so depressed lately," and you tell her she should go see a therapist instead of giving her hope from a biblical basis, what are you saying about your belief in the sufficiency of Scripture?

Having said that, there is a proper place for professional help — from a person who is biblically based and will help deal with the heart issues, while using God's Word to teach Truth as He changes the heart. That person should believe in the sufficiency of Scripture, not in the humanistic theories and methods of popular psychology. Psychology has its place and is very helpful for the study of human behavior, but when it becomes people-centered instead of God-centered, it is no longer helpful for the believer. This is why theology and doctrine matter in One-Another ministry.

Let's let the Scriptures themselves teach this lesson. Please look up the following Scriptures, and make note of what they say to you about God's Word:

*Psalm 119:9

*2 Timothy 3:16-17

*Amos 8:11-12

*Hebrews 1:1-2

*2 Peter 1:20-21

*Isaiah 55:10-11

*Luke 24:44-49

*1 Thessalonians 2:13

*John 17:17

*Revelation 21:5b

*Psalm 33:11

*Psalm 119:89-91

*Isaiah 40:8

*Luke 16:31

*John 5:24

*1 John 5:11-13

*Deuteronomy 32:45-47

*Joshua 1:8

*1 Peter 2:1-3

*2 Peter 1:2-4

In order to be a good friend, mentor, or helper of any kind, it is critical to be a student of the Word yourself. A great goal is to someday take a class in theology and doctrine in order to solidify your beliefs and to wrestle with any questions you have. Or, study it for yourself, including reading what several reputable theology authors have to say on topics.

For now, examine yourself to see if you truly believe in the sufficiency of Scripture to offer hope to others. Be honest about your knowledge of God, His ways, and His Word; admit where you know you are lacking. Ask The Lord to help you to grow in this, so that you will be equipped to offer hope to others.

How do you become equipped?

Get a Bible. Put your hands on it. Put your eyes in it. Wrap your heart around it. Set your mind on it. Study it. Meditate on it. Memorize it. Apply it. Share hope from it with others.

There is a caution to be observed when we are turning to God's Word to offer hope to others. There is a theological term — *eisegesis* — that means that a person misinterprets a verse in such a way that the verse supports a person's own ideas, making the verse say something that it didn't. It can be a temptation to bend Scripture so that it supports your own ideas, opinions, and viewpoints. That is not the purpose of Scripture. We are to conform our lives to God's Word, not conform God's Word to our lives. Let the Bible speak for itself, and let it change your heart and mind. That is why we study it!

In contrast to *eisegesis* is another theological term *exegesis*. *Exegesis* is the explanation or interpretation of Scriptural text. All who claim Jesus Christ as Lord and Savior and believe that His Word is their source of truth and direction can engage in sound *exegesis*. It is not just for scholars and pastors. *Exegesis* is essential to the life of every believer, especially as they engage in One-Another relationships. In order to offer wisdom and truth to help guide other's in their lives, you have to progressively master God's Word by growing in love, knowledge, and application of it day by day. We master God's Word by studying it!

According to Moses, our very lives are dependent on our ability to read, comprehend, and follow instruction from God as provided in His Word. "It is your life." He says in the following verse:

"He said to them, 'Take to heart all the words I have solemnly declared to you this day, so that you may command your children to obey carefully all the words of this law. They are not just idle words for you—they are your life. By them you will live long in the land you are crossing the Jordan to possess.'" (Deuteronomy 32:46-47)

God's Word is LIFE to you!

Additional Notes, Lesson Two: Life On Life, Rooted in God's Word

(Use this for extra homework space and to take notes on our session discussion)

A WORD OF HOPE About Anger and Forgiveness

Remember to APPLY THE GOSPEL and THINK BIBLICALLY as you share hope with One-Another.

You may wonder why we have both anger and forgiveness in the same lesson. More often than not, they go hand in hand. A woman who is unforgiving is an angry woman. An angry woman is unforgiving. The only antidote for anger is forgiveness. The world offers many so-called "solutions" to anger problems. There are anger management courses, medications to calm anger, psychological methods for unleashing your anger, and any number of self-help remedies.

Anger does not always look "angry." It can be expressed outwardly, which is what we most commonly think of when we think about anger. It can also be turned inward, which eventually causes feelings of depression. A depressed woman may not look angry to you, but often when you dig deeper with her and take a look at her heart (her thoughts, beliefs, and desires), you will find an angry woman who has allowed her anger to go unresolved. There is very likely unforgiveness in her heart.

When you are sharing hope with someone with an angry and unforgiving heart, it is critical to review the Gospel with her. Be as certain as you can that she understands it clearly and that she believes it. Then begin to teach her to apply it to her anger and unforgiveness. If after a time you are not seeing any evidence that she is growing in her ability to forgive, you need to consider encouraging her to seek help from a Biblical Counselor.

It is helpful to understand anger and forgiveness accurately before you can offer hope to others. First, let's take a look at anger. Anger is defined as *an emotional response to a perceived wrong*. It is a feeling of outrage when perceiving or thinking about injustice.

Ephesians 4:26-27 tells us not to sin when we are angry. While not all of our anger is sinful, most of it is. Anger is sinful if it results from not getting our way. Self-centeredness is at the center of sinful anger.

"In your anger, do not sin. Do not let the sun go down while you are still angry, and do not give the devil a foothold." (Ephesians 4:26-27)

To express righteous anger, first, we must understand what makes God angry, and, secondly, how God expresses His anger. The Bible tells us all we need to know about this. A big part of our problem is the limited time we spend in God's Word seeking to know Him and live by His Truth.

Psalm 7:11 says, "God is angry with the wicked every day." However, note that whenever the Bible describes God as angry, He remains holy and just. God is slow to anger, yet simultaneously merciful, gracious, compassionate, forgiving, and abundant in lovingkindness and truth — read Psalm 103:8-18. Note primarily that God's anger is ALWAYS directed at rebellion or disobedience to His commands, which are always holy and just and for His glory and our good. Read the following Scriptures: Deuteronomy 29:14-21; Psalm 78:21-22; Romans 2:5; and Hebrews 3:7-11.

As we limit our expressions of anger to God's model, we will find ourselves far less burdened with feelings of vengeance and remorse. Man's sinful, self-centered anger never accomplishes God's purposes (James 1:19-20). It's about Him, not about you or me.

If we have limited our expressions of anger to God's model, we are also far more likely to be forgiving. The following are some statements about forgiveness for you to consider. Use them to evaluate whether or not you are harboring any unforgiveness, and use them to share hope with others.

*The parable in Matthew 18:21-35 teaches us about the nature of love as we forgive others: Forgiveness cancels a debt (this is a metaphor for forgiveness). When there is a debt, someone must pay. Either the one who owes must pay it back, or the one who is owed must absorb the loss.
Forgiveness requires bearing the pain and loss yourself.
Just as Jesus bore our sin as He forgave us on the cross, so must we willingly bear our offender's sin when we forgive them.

*Forgiveness is not a feeling; it is a choice. The feelings of forgiveness come as a result of forgiveness and reconciliation. We are commanded to forgive!

*Forgiveness is totally undeserved. No one deserves it. There is no good work we can do to earn God's forgiveness. Likewise, the person who offended you can never do enough to deserve your forgiveness. God forgave you out of mercy. You must choose to show mercy and forgive in the same manner that you have been forgiven (see Ephesians 4:32).

*Forgiveness is a threefold promise:

1. Forgiveness means that you will not bring up that offense again or use it against them. The only reason to ever bring it up is for the purpose of reconciliation, not vengeance.
2. Forgiveness means that you will not bring it up to others in gossip or malign them because of it. We too often fall into gossip and place all blame on others.
3. Forgiveness means you will not bring it up to yourself and dwell on it. You do not replay the videotape of the sin and you do not savor the details.

*Failure to forgive turns victims into victimizers. When we fail to forgive, we are active, not passive. We want to extract payment until we are satisfied. We take God's place and dole out doses of our own version of justice.

*Forgiveness is both an event, and a process. When we forgive someone, it is an event of "I forgive you." In addition, every time we remember the offense or think about it, we must continue to forgive again and again and again. We must remember the threefold promise we made and we must not act on any sinful desire for revenge.

*If you do not understand forgiveness as an event and a process, discouragement and guilt can set in, and anger lingers. Lingering anger becomes bitterness. This is because the decision to forgive may not immediately eradicate the hurt, lack of trust, and anger you have towards the person. But if you see it as both an event and a process, discouragement and guilt are minimized. You know you HAVE forgiven, even though you are also aware of your temptation to make the person pay. This awareness keeps you vigilant against the sin in your own heart. It leads you to God's strength when you struggle.

*Forgiveness is not forgetting. The word *remember* in Scriptures about forgiveness does not refer to memory, but to the promise not to treat that person as their sins deserve, just like God does not treat us as our sins deserve. He chooses to absorb the cost himself in the person and work of Jesus Christ. We must choose to absorb the cost when we forgive others (see Jeremiah 31:34).

*Forgiving does not mean that you become vulnerable, like a doormat. Scripture does not tell us to make it easy for people to sin against us. It calls us to love them by challenging their actions. There may not always be opportunities for godly confrontation — sometimes we are called to suffer in a godly way — but this confrontation is important. It is a lack of love when we don't take the opportunity to confront in a godly way.

*In dealing with someone who habitually sins against us: Matthew 18:15-17 outlines the steps to take if repentance and reconciliation do not occur. Forgiveness does not mean turning a blind eye to sin. Please read the passage in your Bible.

*We are to love the sinner wisely. Romans 12:17-19 teaches us how to establish boundaries for loving a habitual sinner. In putting this into practice, you are entrusting that sinner to God instead of taking matters in to your own hands. Sometimes others have to be called in to help, and sometimes that may even mean civil authorities for safety, or church leaders for discipline. Forgiving does not make it easy for someone to sin against you.

*Luke 17:3 says to forgive only if the person repents. Mark 11:25 says you must immediately forgive an offender if you recall a sin. BOTH ARE TRUE. One of these describes the vertical axis of forgiveness, the other the horizontal axis of forgiveness.
Mark 11:25 is the vertical: man to God. It is my own heart attitude toward the person before God. It calls me to repent of bitterness, and forgive. Forgiveness as an attitude (vertically) must be present in my heart first.

Luke 17:3 speaks of the horizontal, person to person. Forgiveness as a transaction between two people is possible only if the offender repents, admits sin, and asks for forgiveness. But even if the offender does not repent, the offended person must maintain forgiveness as an attitude in the vertical dimension. You cannot use the offender's failure to seek forgiveness as an excuse to hold on to your anger and hurt!

*We tend to err on the side of not forgiving rather than forgiving. Without the grace of Christ working in us, forgiving does not become part of our lifestyle. Only someone who understands she has been forgiven will routinely forgive others. But none of us will ever forgive others in a measure that equals what God has forgiven us through Christ! When we fail to forgive, we have lost sight of our own forgiven debt.

*Sometimes our own self righteousness keeps us from forgiving. It is as if we don't think we really need to be forgiven, and our hearts have hardened.

*Sometimes we think we are unforgivable. This may sound humble, but it is actually pride. It is as if we are saying, "My sin is so big that God's grace can't even top it!" We also may not want to rely solely on God's mercy because we would rather work for it.

*Sometimes we think God has forgiven us, but that "I just can't forgive myself." This is totally unbiblical thinking. It is God who judges us and pronounces us NOT GUILTY by virtue of our trust in Him. But when we make the statement "forgive myself," we sit as judge and overrule God's decision.

*Sometimes, the joy of His forgiveness has grown dim. We forget about God's grace, and we need to be constantly reminded of it through One-Another relationships and the sacraments of Baptism and the Lord's Supper, Scripture, worship, and prayer.

*FORGIVENESS and ASKING FOR FORGIVENESS are supernatural works of grace. They can only happen when God's forgiveness captivates our hearts!

Grace is getting what you don't deserve. Mercy is not getting what you do deserve. We have a gracious and merciful God. Because of His grace and mercy, let's purpose not to withhold forgiveness as we do Life on Life, One-Another ministry together!

✝ A Word of Hope About Anger and Forgiveness, CASE STUDY:

A woman in your church, Leslie, confesses to you that she is very unhappy in her marriage. You ask her some questions to get a little more of her story. She tells you that five years earlier, her husband had an affair. When he confessed it to her, he sought her forgiveness. He repented and has not returned to that sin. She told him she forgave him, yet she has struggled ever since with a deep feeling of anger and bitterness. She does not express it to him, and she does not express it outwardly. But in her thought life, she is struggling to stop thinking about it, and she admits she still holds it against him in her heart. He is unaware of this, although he does ask her why she seems distant and disinterested in him much of the time. She does not believe in divorce, so she is committed to stay in the marriage, but she says that she is very unhappy. She then admits that she can't stop picturing him with another woman, and she wonders how she compares to that woman. Her thoughts get carried away, and she finds herself growing more and more bitter. How would you help her? What would you say to her as you purpose to share hope from God's Word?

Additional Notes, Lesson Two: A Word of Hope About Anger and Forgiveness

(Use this for extra homework space and to take notes on our session discussion)

APPLYING EPHESIANS 4:32: Forgiveness

Ephesians 4:32

"Be kind and compassionate to one another, forgiving each other, just as in Christ God forgave you."

You will study this most accurately by reading it in context in Ephesians 4:17-32, which is the broader passage that this verse is taken from. Remember that our focus for this study is One-Another ministry so you will want to study that and related themes as you dig in.

Mentor's Bible Study Method Guide

Meditate *Memorize *Meaning *Meet *Master *Mentor

Please refer to the Mentor's Bible Study Method Guide in the Introduction for more details on each step if you wish.

Meditate:

Memorize:

Meaning:

Meet:

Master:

Mentor:

BIBLICAL MENTORS: Paul and Barnabas

Acts 13:2-3

"While they were worshiping the Lord and fasting, the Holy Spirit said, 'Set apart for me Barnabas and Saul for the work to which I have called them.' So after they had fasted and prayed, they placed their hands on them and sent them off."

You will study this One-Another relationship more accurately by reading it throughout the books of Acts 11, Acts 13, and Acts 15. In addition to the verses mentioned above you can understand their relationship more by looking up the other places that their names are mentioned together. Use your Mentor Resource ideas to do this.

Mentor's Bible Study Method Guide

Meditate *Memorize *Meaning *Meet *Master *Mentor

Please refer to the Mentor's Bible Study Method Guide in the Introduction for more details on each step.

<u>Meditate:</u>

Memorize:

Meaning:

Meet:

Master:

Mentor:

Lesson Three

1 Thessalonians 4:18
"Therefore comfort one another with these words."

LIFE ON LIFE, In Your Family

God Himself is the model of relating to family members. God has ordained certain roles in the family, and teaches us in His Word how we are to Biblically treat one another in the context of our family life.

Let's take a look at a Biblical view of the family. Family life today is under attack. The divorce rate is higher than ever before, even in the church. Roles are no longer defined in Biblical terms. There is absenteeism of parents, a breakdown of authority, preoccupation with material things, lack of time together, financial pressures due to a struggling economy, and many other problems. God's Word teaches that the institution of family is of divine origin (Genesis 1:26-27; Genesis 2:7; Genesis 2:21-22). It also teaches that there is divine purpose in it (Genesis 2:18; Matthew 19:4-6; Genesis 1:28; Psalm 127:3-5). The only true hope for recovery of family life is a commitment to the Bible's teachings. Specifically, for our study of One-Another relationships, what does the Bible have to say about our roles in one another's lives?

Ephesians 5:21 calls for the marriage relationship to be characterized by mutual and voluntary submission. Read it in context in Ephesians 5:15-33.

If you are married, look honestly at your own marriage relationship. How well does it line up with what God is teaching us in this passage? What responsibility do you take for this, and what will you do about it? What needs to change, in order for you to be in a healthy One-Another relationship with your husband? If you are not married, please consider this teaching anyway because one day you might be married. You also might disciple a woman who is married.

Commit to submit to God's Word on this matter of submission. If you struggle in this area, it will show in your One-Another ministry to women and girls outside your family as well, because you will not be a good example according to Titus 2:3-5.

"Older women likewise are to be reverent in behavior, not slanderers or slaves to much wine. They are to teach what is good, and so train the young women to love their husbands and children, to be self-controlled, pure, working at home, kind, and submissive to their own husbands, that the word of God may not be reviled." (Titus 2:3-5)

Scripture also teaches us how we, as mothers, are to relate to our children. Write down what each of the following Scriptures have to say about our role as mothers. Again, take an honest look at your personal mothering. If you are not a mother, you will benefit from looking at these verses because you are likely to engage in One-Another relationships with women who are mothers. You may also become a mother someday! Ask the Lord to show you where you are falling short and to help you to mother your children according to God's Word.

*Deuteronomy 6:6-7

*Proverbs 22:6

*Ephesians 6:4

*2 Timothy 1:5

Of course, there are other One-Another relationships within families, with relatives that are not part of your immediate family. As you learn more about the One-Anothers, you will see how the same principles and Truths will apply to your relatives as to anyone else that God places in your life.

You may have often heard it said that we should prioritize our lives something like this:

God first.
Husband second.
Children third.
Career fourth.
Church/ministry fifth.
Friends and relatives sixth.

There are varying versions of this concept, with Scriptures that seems to support it (sometimes *eisegesis*, sometimes *exegesis*). The problem with a list like this is that it implies that if you run out of time or energy before getting to the bottom of the priority list, then it's ok to just forego that priority. Where is that supported in Scripture? It isn't.

There is another way of looking at this idea of prioritizing God and people. 1 John 3:23 indicates that we can't love God and not love people, and we can't love people if we don't love God. It is not a matter of prioritizing; it is a matter of love. This concept is backed up by every single One-Another verse or passage in Scripture. This is a better way of viewing our Christian priorities:

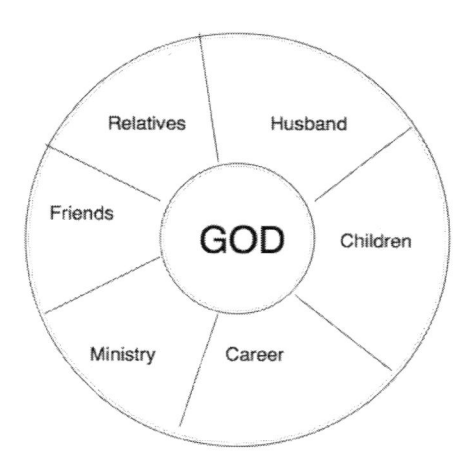

God is at the center of everything, and anything else in life flows from His presence in our lives through the indwelling of His Holy Spirit. We cannot have Biblical One-Another relationships without a relationship first with God. We cannot have a relationship with God and avoid having relationship with each other. Everything we have — family, career, ministry, friends —are gifts from God, and we are to be stewards over them. Psalm 8:4-8 reminds us that God made everything and He owns everything, but we have responsibility for caring for what He gave us.

"4 what is man that you are mindful of him,
  the son of man that you care for him?
5 You made him a little lower than the heavenly beings

and crowned him with glory and honor.

 6 You made him ruler over the works of your hands;
   you put everything under his feet:
7 all flocks and herds,
   and the beasts of the field,
8 the birds of the air,
   and the fish of the sea,
   all that swim the paths of the seas" (Psalm 8:4-8).

As you minister in One-Another relationships with your family, be sure that you are not neglecting one area of the God-centered circle of priorities for the sake of the other. It is not a matter of prioritizing; it is a matter of stewardship of your time, energy, resources, and gifts. The emphasis you are able to place in any given area will change according to the season of life you are in, but none of the areas are meant to be ignored entirely. God does not assign you activities or people in order to overwhelm you. If you are overwhelmed and unable to have a healthy One-Another lifestyle in your family, either you are taking on things that are not from Him in the first place, or you are not stewarding them well.

Take a few moments to evaluate your family relationships. Ask God to reveal to you anything that hinders you from managing your lifestyle to His glory. Write down any thoughts here.

Additional Notes, Lesson Three: Life On Life, In Your Family

(Use this for extra homework space and to take notes on our session discussion)

A WORD OF HOPE About Worry, Fear, Anxiety and Stress

~~~~~~

Remember to APPLY THE GOSPEL and THINK BIBLICALLY as you share hope with One-Another.

Anxiety — along with fear, worry, and stress — are things that all human beings struggle with. They are closely related; therefore, in this lesson we will put them all under the term "anxiety." Anxiety takes on various forms, and people's responses to it take on various forms. Anxiety is *the prolonged sensation of fear in response to a perceived threat against oneself.* Fear, by definition, is *a self-protective tool to help a person sense and respond to a perceived danger.* We see this in Psalm 55:3-6.

" 3 My enemies shout at me,
   making loud and wicked threats.
  They bring trouble on me
   and angrily hunt me down.

4 My heart pounds in my chest.
   The terror of death assaults me.
5 Fear and trembling overwhelm me,
   and I can't stop shaking.
6 Oh, that I had wings like a dove;
   then I would fly away and rest!" (Psalm 55:3-6 NLT)

From the Psalmist's viewpoint, he is anxious due to threats from the enemy. He is terrified of death and danger, and he perceives escape to be the best solution. This passage is a vivid example of what some might call an "anxiety attack" or "panic attack."

While it is a common human experience to be anxious, it can be debilitating. We must think Biblically about anxiety so that it will not interfere in our relationships, damage our ability to engage in daily activities, or consume our thought life. It is natural to feel worried or troubled about things in life that are indeed worrisome or troubling! It is not God's will or plan for you, however, to be so consumed with it that it overtakes your trust in the Lord.

Note: Anxiety that brings on a panic attack is serious, and this would be an appropriate time to urge someone to seek Biblical Counseling. The counselor is trained for and skilled to know how to best advise someone like this. Often, she will require a medical evaluation to rule out any physiological causes, and to evaluate for the appropriateness of medication. Although it is true that medications tend to be over-prescribed in many situations, it can at times be a useful tool that can stop the effect of excessive fear and anxiety while the heart issues are dealt with through Biblical Counseling. When the counseling is effective, the medication can quite often be stopped.

Let's take a look at the difference between a person who has debilitating anxiety, and the person who sometimes feels anxious but her trust in God keeps her from an overriding anxiety. Look up the following verses, and write down what they say to us about how to deal with our stress, worry, fear and anxiety:

*Isaiah 26:3

*Philippians 4:6-7

*Matthew 6:25-34

*Romans 8:32

*1 Corinthians 10:13

*Romans 12:2

*Philippians 2:20

*1 Peter 5:7

*1 Thessalonians 5:18

*Philippians 4:12

*1 Timothy 6:6-8

This is not an exhaustive list! Can you think of other verses that speak to how we should deal with our anxieties? List them here:

As you share hope with someone who is anxious, encourage her to look at her worries and fears at the heart level. What is she thinking, believing, and desiring that is feeding such anxiety? Remind her to think Biblically about these things.

✝ A Word of Hope About Worry, Fear, Anxiety and Stress, CASE STUDY:

Sherry is a woman who just started attending your church. You notice that she sits by herself and rarely smiles. Her expression strikes you as worried and fretful much of the time. You approach her to introduce yourself, and she hesitantly says hello. You invite her for coffee that week. As you chat, she begins to tell you her story. She is a single mom who has never been married. Her son is in special education in the third grade. He has a form of autism, and his symptoms are gradually worsening. She is struggling to make ends meet on her income as a grocery store clerk. She is able to have her son stay for an after-school daycare program while she works, but she feels that it is not structured enough for him. He is getting bigger and more difficult to manage each year. He has violent outbursts and often does not sleep well at night. She worries about his future — what does his future hold and who will take care of him if something happens to her? How will she have enough money for his care if she can no longer handle him by herself? She believes in God and says that she has trusted in Jesus as her Savior, but she wonders why He allows such a struggle in her and her son's lives? Why would He allow her son to suffer so much? Why would He not provide a husband for her someday to love her and her son and to ease her loneliness? Does God really care about her? She has far more questions than answers, and she is obviously reaching out for some help, encouragement, and hope. How would you offer hope to this woman in the context of this conversation? What might you do to help her as time goes on?

Additional Notes, Lesson Three: A Word of Hope About Worry, Fear, Anxiety, and Stress

(Use this for extra homework space and to take notes on our session discussion)

APPLYING 1 THESSALONIANS 4:18: Comfort

1 Thessalonians 4:18

"Therefore comfort one another with these words." (NASB)

You will study this most accurately by reading in context in 1 Thessalonians 4:13-18, which is the broader passage that this verse is taken from. Remember that our focus for this study is One-Another ministry, so you will want to study that and related themes as you dig in.

Mentor's Bible Study Method Guide

*Meditate *Memorize *Meaning *Meet *Master *Mentor*

Please refer to the Mentor's Bible Study Method Guide in the Introduction for more details on each step if you wish.

<u>Meditate:</u>

Memorize:

Meaning:

Meet:

Master:

Mentor:

BIBLICAL MENTORS: Paul and Timothy

2 Timothy 2:1-7

"**1** You then, my son, be strong in the grace that is in Christ Jesus. **2** And the things you have heard me say in the presence of many witnesses entrust to reliable people who will also be qualified to teach others. **3** Join with me in suffering, like a good soldier of Christ Jesus. **4** No one serving as a soldier gets entangled in civilian affairs, but rather tries to please his commanding officer. **5** Similarly, anyone who competes as an athlete does not receive the victor's crown except by competing according to the rules. **6** The hardworking farmer should be the first to receive a share of the crops. **7** Reflect on what I am saying, for the Lord will give you insight into all this."

You will study this One-Another relationship more accurately by reading it throughout the books of 1 Timothy and 2 Timothy. In addition to the verses mentioned above, you can understand their relationship more by looking up the other places that their names are mentioned together. Use your Mentor Resource ideas to do this.

Mentor's Bible Study Method Guide

*Meditate *Memorize *Meaning *Meet *Master *Mentor*

Please refer to the Mentor's Bible Study Method Guide in the Introduction for more details on each step.

<u>Meditate:</u>

Memorize:

Meaning:

Meet:

Master:

Mentor:

Lesson Four

Galatians 5:13
"You, my brothers, were called to be free. But do not use your freedom to indulge the sinful nature; rather, serve one another in love."

LIFE ON LIFE in a Culture of Soulcare in the Local Church

The church is called the "pillar and support of the truth" by Paul. The truth of God's Word has been preserved and disseminated throughout the ages by the church. All people desiring to grow in the knowledge of the truth and to learn more about God should find a local church that honors and teaches the Bible and begin to benefit from the teaching ministry which is offered there for them by God.

"Although I hope to come to you soon, I am writing you these instructions so that, if I am delayed, you will know how people ought to conduct themselves in God's household, which is the church of the living God, the pillar and foundation of the truth." (1 Timothy 3:14-15)

Life On Life, One-Another ministry is best done in the context of your local church. If we take an honest look at our churches in our lifetime, we have to admit that we have often neglected to care for the souls of our church family in this context.

Take a moment to reflect on your experience with local churches in your life. How many have you been to? Were your experiences positive or negative, or both? Why? Write down anything these questions stir in you.

Now take a look at those same church experiences from your life (including your present one), and think about how One-Another ministry was/is portrayed there. Is there a culture of caring for each other? Are people being mentored; specifically, are women engaging in Titus 2 style of ministry with other women and girls? Is there ongoing discipleship in the form of expository preaching, small groups and/or Bible studies, Sunday School programs, or other similar opportunities? Are new believers discipled in the basics of the faith? Is there a Biblical Counseling ministry or something similar? How are people who are struggling with serious problems helped? Are all members encouraged to serve one another and their community? Jot down some of your thoughts about this.

The apostle Paul explained that the church was the "body of Christ" with Jesus as its "head."

"And God placed all things under his feet and appointed him to be head over everything for the church, which is his body, the fullness of him who fills everything in every way." (Ephesians 1:22-23)

Paul's description emphasizes the relationship that each believer and the local church has to Jesus. Since the church is a living organism consisting of people who believe in and follow their Savior Jesus Christ, they are under His rule, and He works through them. Anyone wanting to draw closer to Jesus and experience His working in their lives will greatly benefit from coming into association with a local body of believers.

God's Word instructs believers not to neglect getting together with other believers. Our purpose as One-Another ministers is to fulfill the Great Commandment and the Great Commission, both within our churches and in our spheres of influence outside the church. Without the local church to edify, encourage, and equip believers, this purpose cannot be fulfilled.

"Let us not give up meeting together, as some are in the habit of doing, but let us encourage one another—and all the more as you see the Day approaching." (Hebrews 10:25)

One-Another ministry is the healthiest when done in the context of the local church whenever possible. You might have many other One-Another relationships outside of your local church body as well, but in this lesson we are dealing primarily with the type of One-Another ministry in a local church that provides for the "soulcare" of individuals.

What do we mean by *soulcare*? It is not a new concept. It was established in the New Testament church in Acts 2.

Please look up Acts 2:42-47 in your Bible, and answer the following questions.

*What priorities of the devoted believers do you see in this passage?

*What attitudes do you see in these believers?

The care that believers had for one another in Acts 2 has continued in various forms through the years. It can be defined as "believers speaking the Truth in love anchored in the Word of God, depending on the Holy Spirit." In our culture, it is called by many names such as:
*Discipling
*Mentoring
*Teaching
*Biblical Counseling
*Pastoral Counseling
*Spiritual Guidance
*Spiritual Formation
*Friendship
*Spiritual Friendship

A church with a culture of soulcare will bear much fruit. Whatever form the church's One-Another ministry takes, it must be rooted in God's Word, exalt Jesus Christ, be empowered by the Holy Spirit, and be loving. Soulcare ministry aims to produce salvation, sanctification, and Spiritual fruit. This is achieved through admonishment, teaching, exhortation, encouragement, comfort, and forbearance.

All believers need soulcare, not just those who are struggling. We all need One-Another ministry in various forms. We do have a tendency in our churches today to neglect the hurting believer. Hurting individuals should be taken care of primarily by the local church, but are often referred out to secular sources of help that will not provide true soulcare. Those sources can have some benefit for learning some behavior management that brings some relief, but they will not provide what we see in our definition of soulcare — "speaking the Truth in love anchored in the Word of God, depending on the Holy Spirit." For a believer to have lasting change and hope, she must be helped with some form of soulcare, preferably within her local church. The next best choice would be help from a local Biblically-based counseling ministry. Biblical Counselors are glad to provide counseling to those who come to them from other churches, but all of them would agree that the best scenario would be that local churches become well equipped to counsel, disciple, mentor, teach, and befriend their own church family.

Please realize that there is occasionally an appropriate time for someone to seek Biblical help outside of their local church. If someone's problems are serious enough that they are seeking counseling, the only option may be an outside Biblical Counselor who can help for a season. The counselor's goal will be to return the woman to her local church for further discipleship once the counseling has ended. If a person is in need of medical assistance or medication, that has to be addressed by a licensed professional. Even if that is the case, she will need good One-Another relationships in her church family as she undergoes whatever kind of treatment she and her doctor choose.

Let's caution against creating an environment in our churches where all we talk about are our struggles and problems, but let's also provide opportunities for hurting people (aren't we all hurting at some time or other?) to get the soulcare they need, through excellent One-Another relationships.

As we proceed in our study, you will begin to discern when the time may be appropriate to refer a woman or girl to counseling or medical care. However, this is not the most common scenario. Most of the time, you will be able to help someone Life On Life with the equipping tools we are learning about through the course of our study of the One-Anothers. While it is true that there is great need for Biblical Counseling, quite often an equipped Biblical Mentor will be able to provide the soulcare that someone needs, Life On Life.

Paul explains that gifted people have been given to the church in order to bring believers to a place of fruitfulness in service and maturity.

"It was he who gave some to be apostles, some to be prophets, some to be evangelists, and some to be pastors and teachers, to prepare God's people for works of service, so that the body of Christ may be built up until we all reach unity in the faith and in the knowledge of the Son of God and become mature, attaining to the whole measure of the fullness of Christ." (Ephesians 4:11-13)

We often say that someone is "called to full-time ministry." True, some believers engage in ministry vocationally, but does that mean that other believers are not engaging in ministry? Of course not. We are all full-time ministers, or we are not ministering at all. You, too, are called to full-time ministry. We all are. One-Another relationships are a ministry, and the lifestyle of a believer. We all are given different gifts useful to specific types of One-Another ministry, but everyone has a ministry of soulcare. That soulcare ministry is at its best in the context of the local church.

Where do you fit in? How do you see yourself gifted for One-Another ministry? Are you confident about your ability to minister to women and girls? What are your insecurities about it? Take some time to talk with the Lord about how He wants to use you in Life On Life relationships in your local church.

As you do Life On Life in the context of your church, be sure to help others to engage in the opportunities the church provides for their ongoing growth. Let's encourage one another to worship, fellowship, prayer, devotion, study, memorization, service, and discipleship.

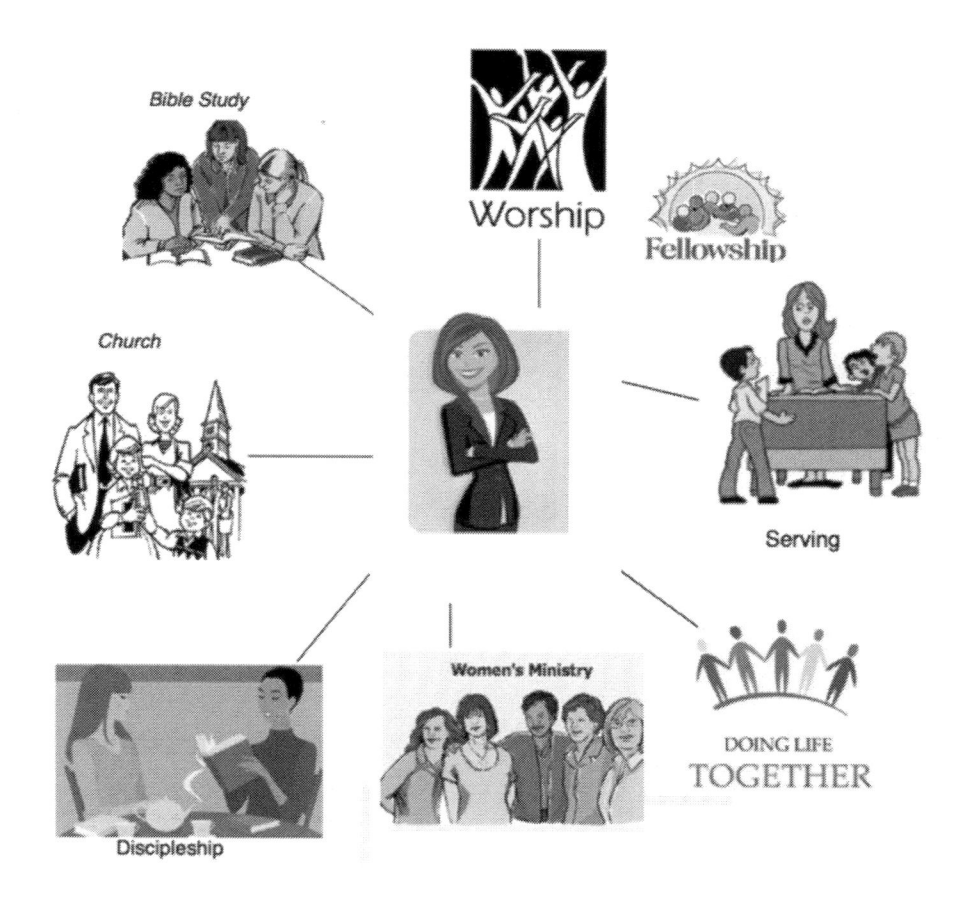

Life On Life, One-Another Ministry!

Additional Notes, Lesson Four: Life On Life in a Culture of Soulcare in the Local Church

(Use this for extra homework space and to take notes on our session discussion)

A WORD OF HOPE About Depression

Remember to APPLY THE GOSPEL and THINK BIBLICALLY as you share hope with One-Another.

Depression is a very common reason that women and girls seek counseling and medical care. There is debate these days about whether or not depression is a physical problem, an emotional problem, or a spiritual problem. From a Biblical standpoint, we do not need to spend much time on these debates, because ultimately the Bible still has what a depressed woman needs for her wellbeing. Whether or not you and she agree that she has a chemical imbalance, hormonal problem, or other physical cause for her depression is not the main concern. Our main concern as we do Life On Life, One-Another ministry with others is that they apply the Gospel and think Biblically. They can learn more about God and His Word and how it applies to their lives regardless of their diagnosis, medication need, emotional problem, or spiritual problem.

It is always critical for a woman dealing with depression to seek medical care. It is important to rule out serious medical issues that can cause hormonal and chemical imbalances. In cases where there is legitimate physical cause, medical care is very appropriate. Where there is no physical cause, it is up to the individual whether or not she chooses a medication treatment. There is a caution in this because medications are so easily obtained and overly prescribed. More often than not, a depressed woman with no medical cause for her depression can benefit and work through her depression with solid Biblical Counseling by a trained counselor or a well equipped mentor.

Depression is extremely common among females. It is not a sign of weakness or spiritual lacking — it is a sign of being human! Some signs that you are depressed are:
 *Unable to sleep
 *A desire to sleep too much and/or fatigue
 *Headaches, body aches, change of appetite
 *An overwhelming sense of sadness and hopelessness
 *A preoccupation with the way you feel
 *Indifference to the things of God

*Finding little or no enjoyment in activities that you previously have enjoyed
*Focusing on your circumstances more than trusting God
*Wishful thinking — wishing your life was different
*Inability to see any purpose in suffering
*Prolonged grieving
*Feeling like a failure
*Suppressed anger — anger turned inward becomes depression

Depression is often marked by the following:
*Regret about the past
*Helplessness about the present
*Hopelessness about the future

What do the following verses have to say about the realities of life in this world?

*James 4:14 —

*Psalm 31:10 —

*Romans 3:23 —

*Romans 3:9 —

*John 15:5 —

*Psalm 142:3-4 —

*Psalm 120:5-7 —

*1 Corinthians 15:30-32 —

*Genesis 3:17 —

*Ecclesiastes 4:8 —

*1 Samuel 25:21 —

*Psalm 73:13-14

It is helpful for us to accept these realities in order to deal honestly and compassionately with people living with depression. Each of us is vulnerable to suffer depression at any time, and it can be helpful initially to simply empathize.

Perhaps you have struggled with depression. If so, what kinds of remedies have you tried, and did they bring lasting relief? (You will not be asked to share these particular answers, this is for your private introspection only.) Are you currently struggling with depression? If so, is it interfering in your daily routines, and what are you doing about it? If this describes you, please don't hesitate to ask for some Biblical help.

As helpful as empathy can be, it is critical to help someone who is depressed to find hope.

It is always helpful to encourage someone who is depressed to read the Psalms. In them, you find empathy and also hope as the Psalmist works through his pain realizing God is sovereign, faithful, and trustworthy.

Hopelessness indicates that there is a problem in the heart, in thoughts, beliefs, or desires. When we dwell on or long for the wrong things, we will feel depressed. God's Word offers many reasons for hopefulness. What do the following verses have to say about hopefulness?

*1 Timothy 1:1

*1 Peter 1:3

*1 John 3:2

*Revelation 22:5

*Psalm 42

Depression is always self-centered. Depressed women need to be encouraged to worship God and appreciate His goodness. It is also helpful to encourage them to serve within their church ministries, so that they, too, are engaging in Life On Life, One-Another ministry.

If you are in a One-Another relationship with a depressed woman who is having great difficulty functioning in her daily routine, that is the time to help her to find a counselor. If her depression is mild with a general sense of sadness and malaise, but she is able to carry out her daily routines, you can help her by sharing a hope with her and walking alongside her, Life On Life.

☦ A Word of Hope About Depression, CASE STUDY:

Elizabeth, a 34 year old wife and mother of three is in your small group. Her husband is not a believer, but he is supportive of her church attendance and allows his children to go to church and Sunday School as well. Elizabeth has not been present at your small group for the past three weeks, and you are wondering why. You run in to Elizabeth at the grocery store, and she looks tired, unkempt, and frazzled and says that she has just been too tired to go to church lately. You ask her why she is so tired, and she says she doesn't really know. She then tells you that she feels like a failure because she can't seem to find joy in anything anymore, and doesn't feel like getting up in the morning. She is getting up and going about her daily business anyway, for the sake of her children, she says. She admits that she is not reading her Bible anymore, and she has not felt like praying. She tells you that her husband suggested she go back to church because he notices a difference in her when she does. She admits that he is frustrated with her change of behavior and doesn't know how to help her. She appreciates his concern, but says that he is not one that she can talk to about things that are bothering her. How could you reach out to Elizabeth and help her?

Additional Notes, Lesson Four: A Word of Hope About Depression

(Use this for extra homework space and to take notes on our session discussion)

APPLYING GALATIANS 5:13: Servanthood

Galatians 5:13

"You, my brothers, were called to be free. But do not use your freedom to indulge the sinful nature; rather, serve one another in love."

You will study this most accurately by reading in context in Galatians 5:1-15, which is the broader passage that this verse is taken from. Remember that our focus for this study is One-Another ministry, so you will want to study that and related themes as you dig in.

Mentor's Bible Study Method Guide

*Meditate *Memorize *Meaning *Meet *Master *Mentor*

Please refer to the Mentor's Bible Study Method Guide in the Introduction for more details on each step if you wish.

<u>Meditate:</u>

Memorize:

Meaning:

Meet:

Master:

Mentor:

BIBLICAL MENTORS: Naomi and Ruth

Ruth 1:16-18

"But Ruth replied, 'Don't urge me to leave you or to turn back from you. Where you go I will go, and where you stay I will stay. Your people will be my people and your God my God. Where you die I will die, and there I will be buried. May the LORD deal with me, be it ever so severely, if anything but death separates you and me.' When Naomi realized that Ruth was determined to go with her, she stopped urging her."

You will study this One-Another relationship more accurately by reading the whole book of Ruth, although the immediate context is in Ruth 1:1-22. In addition to the verses mentioned above, you can understand their relationship more by looking up the other places that their names are mentioned together. Use your Mentor Resource ideas to do this.

Mentor's Bible Study Method Guide

*Meditate *Memorize *Meaning *Meet *Master *Mentor*

Please refer to the Mentor's Bible Study Method Guide in the Introduction for more details on each step.

<u>Meditate:</u>

Memorize:

Meaning:

Meet:

Master:

Mentor:

Lesson Five

James 5:16
"Therefore confess your sins to each other and pray for each other so that you may be healed. The prayer of a righteous man is powerful and effective."

LIFE ON LIFE: Prayer

It is critical that a deep prayer life be a part of every believer who is engaging in Life On Life, One-Another relationships. It is a profound gift that you can give someone, whether they know you are praying for them or not. It is a powerful way to love one another. As we do Life On Life together, we should be praying together and encouraging each other to have a healthy prayer life. We must also be in regular prayer for those women and girls we are mentoring, discipling, and helping.

God's Word says that we are not fighting a human battle, but a spiritual one.

"For our struggle is not against flesh and blood, but against the rulers, against the authorities, against the powers of this dark world and against the spiritual forces of evil in the heavenly realms." (Ephesians 6:12)

God has given us His armor, and our job is to wear it!

"Put on the full armor of God so that you can take your stand against the devil's schemes." (Ephesians 6:11)

We not only must wear this armor, but we need to teach and remind one another to do the same. Any time you are ministering to another believer, there will be spiritual warfare. Satan is after us whenever the Gospel is being proclaimed and applied. He will attack us in our efforts to have healthy One-Another relationships.

Read Ephesians 6:10-18 and list all of the pieces of the armor of God:

"And pray in the Spirit on all occasions with all kinds of prayers and requests. With this in mind, be alert and always keep on praying for all the saints." (Verse 18) We cannot take this lightly. If we look closely at this one verse that wraps up the passage about the armor we are to wear, we will find some key concepts about how to pray in our One-Another relationships. What do each of these phrases mean in regards to your One-Another prayer life?

* "pray in the Spirit" —

* "on all occasions" —

* "all kinds of prayers" —

* "be alert" —

* "always keep on praying" —

* "for the saints" —

How is your prayer life? We should be asking one another this question often.

What are the hindrances to a healthy prayer life?

How can you encourage others in their prayer lives?

How do these verses speak about prayer and having a healthy prayer life?

*Psalm 141:2

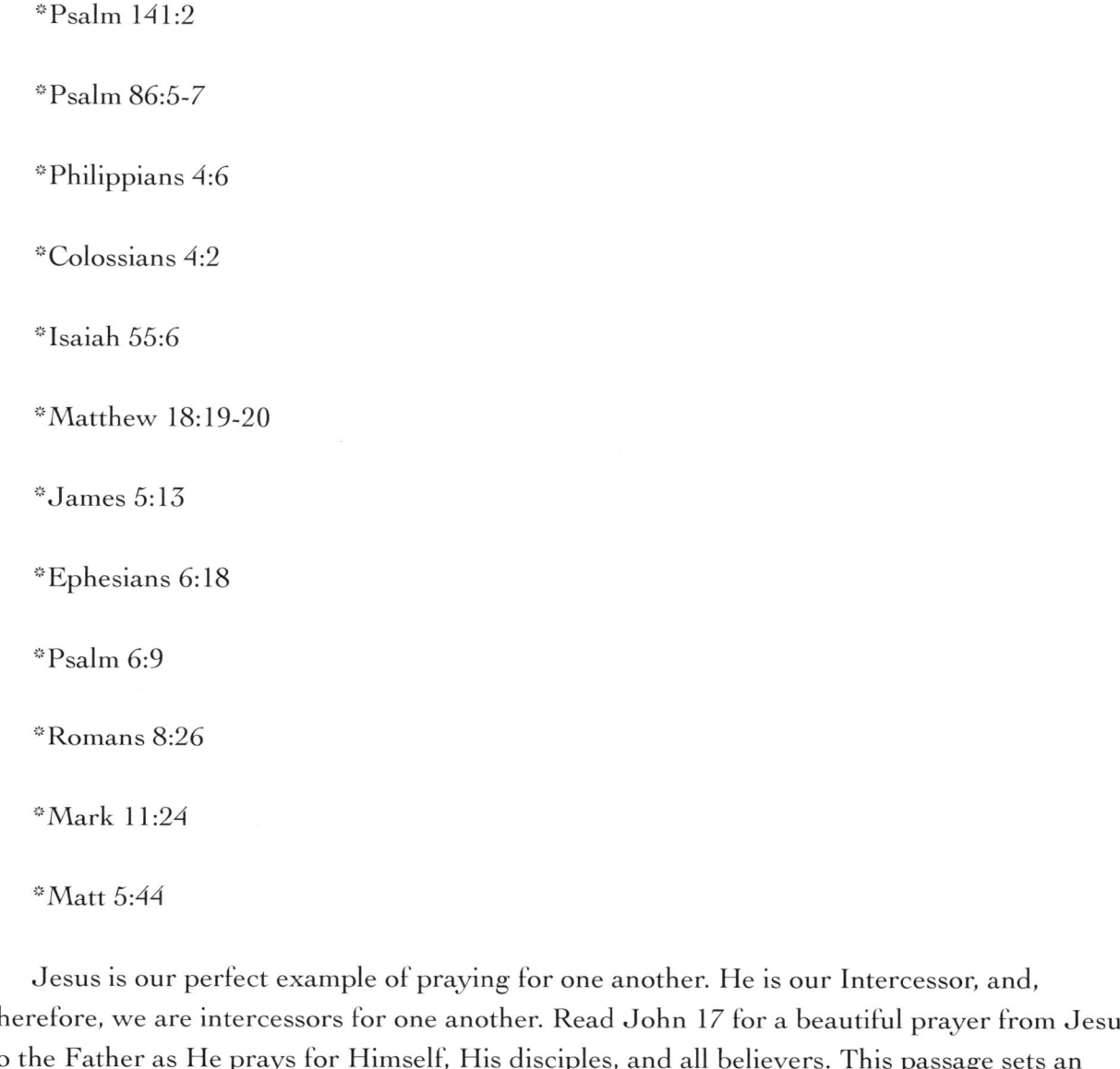

*Psalm 86:5-7

*Philippians 4:6

*Colossians 4:2

*Isaiah 55:6

*Matthew 18:19-20

*James 5:13

*Ephesians 6:18

*Psalm 6:9

*Romans 8:26

*Mark 11:24

*Matt 5:44

Jesus is our perfect example of praying for one another. He is our Intercessor, and, therefore, we are intercessors for one another. Read John 17 for a beautiful prayer from Jesus to the Father as He prays for Himself, His disciples, and all believers. This passage sets an example for us as we pray for ourselves, those we are ministering to, and all believers.

How does John 17 challenge you in your own prayer life?

Prayer is all about intimacy and communication with the Father. It is His ministry to us! All relationships require communication. When we neglect our prayer lives, we are neglecting our relationship with Him entirely. God wants this relationship, and He knows we need what He can give. Through prayer, we are transformed and renewed with intimacy with the Creator of the universe. Without this intimacy, we have no means for a healthy and fruitful ministry.

Prayer, alongside God's Word, is a very powerful Life On Life, One-Another tool. We need to understand the importance of prayer, the power of prayer, and the impact of prayer on our relationships as revealed in the following statements.

1. God reveals Himself to us through prayer as we learn more about His character and how His perfect will is working itself out in our own life. When our understanding of God is deeper, our faith and desire to worship Him grows. Read Psalm 143:10.

2. God invites us to bring our burdens to Him. Our Heavenly Father is able to bring victory to any challenge we face. He is our spiritual, emotional, and physical Healer. Read Matthew 11:28.

3. God responds to the prayers of His people. It is through prayer that His work is accomplished on earth. Prayer is vital to any success. Read James 5:16.

4. God imparts wisdom and understanding through prayer. We can rest in His omniscience and avail ourselves of His counsel. Read James 1:5.

5. God exercises His authority and ability to do the impossible through the prayers of believers. We can have confidence in taking requests to our mighty Lord. Read Matthew 21:22.

6. God extends His power to us through prayer so that we can resist temptation. With prayer, we always have a shield of protection available. Read Matthew 26:41.

Commit today to engaging in a powerful prayer life, and encourage others to do the same!

Additional Notes, Lesson Five — Life On Life: Prayer

(Use this for extra homework space and to take notes on our session discussion)

A WORD OF HOPE About Grief and Loss

Remember to APPLY THE GOSPEL and THINK BIBLICALLY as you share hope with One-Another.

We are going to encounter girls and women who are suffering from loss and grief from time to time. There are many types of loss, and each type brings its own form of grief. We also all grieve in different ways. Let's throw out the psychological and traditional wisdom that says that grief "comes in stages," as if it is some sort of formula to be followed. That tends to make us feel as if we are not grieving properly if we are not following that formula. That formula is not found in Scripture, although grief is evident all throughout Scripture. God's Word shows us how we are to view it Biblically, and how we can minister to those who are grieving and suffering loss of various kinds.

In order to have a proper theology of grief, we need to again apply the Gospel and encourage those who are grieving to do the same.

Hebrews 6:19 reminds us that in our trials, we are anchored to God's love.

"We have this hope as an anchor for the soul, firm and secure. It enters the inner sanctuary behind the curtain…"

Isaiah 12:2-3 reminds us that we have a deep, deep well to draw from. The well of salvation!

"Surely God is my salvation;
  I will trust and not be afraid.
The LORD, the LORD, is my strength and my song;
  he has become my salvation."
With joy you will draw water
  from the wells of salvation." (Isaiah 12:2-3)

A woman or girl who is grieving, especially in the early hours and days of a loss, will respond best to simple comfort in the form of your presence, a hug, crying with her, helping her with a meal or housework, or just sitting with her. We often try to use our words too soon, when her emotions are too raw and she is not ready to receive them. Ask God to lead you by His Spirit as you minister to someone who is grieving. A good practice is that it is better to say nothing and just be present than to say all the wrong things.

Have you ever had someone try to comfort you in your grief, only to find that their words were not helpful or comforting, even though you know they meant well? What are some things people say that might be better left unsaid during the early moments of grief?

After some time has passed — maybe a funeral has come and gone, life around her is returning to normal and the impact of her loss is now really hitting her — you have some new opportunities for sharing a Word of hope with her. Now she will be ready to receive the comfort you can offer her from God's Word.

We are called to offer hope to those who have suffered a loss and are grieving. "Rejoice with those who rejoice; mourn with those who mourn." (Romans 12:15)

Help someone apply the Gospel to their grief by reminding them that God is the source of all comfort.

*In Genesis 6:6, God reveals that He grieves over our sin. God knows grief.

*In Matthew 26:37-44, Jesus asked several times that His burden be removed, while still submitting Himself to the Father's will. When we grieve, we feel that the pain is too much to bear. Jesus understands.

*In John 11:17-44, Jesus grieves with others. We are called to grieve with others, too.

*Revelation 21:4 offers us the future hope of heaven. In our grief, we need to remember that this fallen earth is not our home.

*He gave His only begotten Son, so that those who believe in Him will have eternal life in heaven (John 3:16). The sacrifice of His own Son caused an unimaginable grief. This is how God can meet us in our own grief — because He understands and has suffered with us and for us.

Most of us have suffered some form of loss and grief in our lifetimes. God wastes nothing, and He will use everything we go through for His glory. Often, our grief will reveal God to us in a fresh, new way. We can then pass on the comfort we have received to others. This is One-

Another ministry!

"Praise be to the God and Father of our Lord Jesus Christ, the Father of compassion and the God of all comfort, who comforts us in all our troubles, so that we can comfort those in any trouble with the comfort we ourselves have received from God." (2 Corinthians 1:3-4)

✝ A Word of Hope About Grief and Loss, CASE STUDY:

Christy is a woman in your small group at church. She has not been attending long, so you don't know her more than superficially at this point. She is 45 years old and the mother of two teenagers. She has shared with the group that she has been a believer for 15 years, and she has served the Lord as a Children's Church worker for several years. As far as you can tell, she appears to be solid and mature in her faith. You have received news on your church prayer chain that her husband was killed in a car accident that morning. None of the other women in your small group are available to minister to her that day, so your pastor has asked that you place a phone call and try to visit with her in person. He has already visited with her himself, but feels that it would be helpful for a woman to reach out to her too. After you call her, she agrees to receive you in to her home that afternoon. She is in the company of her children and a couple of friends, but her family has not yet arrived from out of town. You walk into the home to find the friends offering comfort to her children, while she sits on the couch crying by herself. How would you minister to her in this moment? After a few weeks have passed, how might your ministry to her change, and how would you offer her hope from God's Word?

Additional Notes, Lesson Five: A Word of Hope About Grief and Loss

(Use this for extra homework space and to take notes on our session discussion)

APPLYING JAMES 5:16: Prayer

James 5:16

"Therefore confess your sins to each other and pray for each other so that you may be healed. The prayer of a righteous man is powerful and effective."

You will study this most accurately by reading in context in James 5:13-20, which is the broader passage that this verse is taken from. Remember that our focus for this study is One-Another ministry, so you will want to study that and related themes as you dig in.

Mentor's Bible Study Method Guide

*Meditate *Memorize *Meaning *Meet *Master *Mentor*

Please refer to the Mentor's Bible Study Method Guide in the Introduction for more details on each step if you wish.

<u>Meditate</u>:

<u>Memorize</u>:

Meaning:

Meet:

Master:

Mentor:

BIBLICAL MENTORS: Elijah and Elisha

2 Kings 2:9

"When they had crossed, Elijah said to Elisha, 'Tell me, what can I do for you before I am taken from you?' 'Let me inherit a double portion of your spirit,' Elisha replied."

You will study this One-Another relationship more accurately by reading about Elijah and Elisha in both 1 Kings and 2 Kings, although the immediate context is in 2 Kings 2:1-18. In addition to the verses mentioned above, you can understand their relationship more by looking up the other places that their names are mentioned together. Use your Mentor Resource ideas to do this.

Mentor's Bible Study Method Guide

*Meditate *Memorize *Meaning *Meet *Master *Mentor*

Please refer to the Mentor's Bible Study Method Guide in the Introduction for more details on each step.

<u>Meditate:</u>

Memorize:

Meaning:

Meet:

Master:

Mentor:

Lesson Six

Hebrews 10:24
"Let us not give up meeting together, as some are in the habit of doing, but let us encourage one another—and all the more as you see the Day approaching."

LIFE ON LIFE in Friendship

"A man of many companions may come to ruin, but there is a friend who sticks closer than a brother." (Proverbs 18:24) An ideal relationship for doing Life On Life, One-Another ministry is in our friendships. We were not made to do life alone, and we need healthy friendships in our lives. It is important to remember that friendships may come and go, but there is that One friend who sticks closer than a brother — Jesus Christ. He is to be central in our relationships with friends.

Life On Life relationships are often done in the context of friendship. In a close friendship, mentoring and discipling are often mutual. Close Christian friends are often fairly equal in their spiritual maturity, and therefore can pour in to each other's lives mutually and equally. When one friend struggles, the other offers her encouragement and hope, and vice versa. There is an equal give and take as the One-Anothers of Scripture are applied in the relationship.

In a more formal mentoring or discipling relationship, there may also be a friendship, but it will be less mutual. The mentor will do the teaching, discipling, and counseling, and the mentee will be the recipient. Of course, there are times that the mentee will be the one to apply a One-Another concept to her mentor, but, in general, it is the other way around.

Females seem to be especially wired for close friendships. We are, by nature, very social and relational. In Ecclesiastes 4:9-10, God tells us, "Two are better than one, because they have a good return for their work: If one falls down, his friend can help him up. But pity the man who falls and has no one to help him up!" Friendship enriches our lives in many ways. What are some ways that your close friendships enrich your life?

Friendships can also present challenges if we are not applying the One-Anothers of Scripture well. If we are self-centered in the relationship, or if we are not engaged in the friendship with the right motives, conflict will be inevitable. What are some of the struggles you have had or currently have in your close friendships?

The book of Proverbs gives us many brief, memorable phrases regarding wise instruction for godly living. This kind of instruction promotes the knowledge of what is right and the strength to live it. The book is permeated with divine counsel. Proverbs touches many concerns that confront the person's desire to live a righteous life. One of these concerns is "friendships." As we can see in Proverbs, friends can either be a positive influence or a spiritual hindrance. God's Word tells us how we are to view our close friendships, so that Christ and His Gospel will be our motive for relationships.

How do the following Scriptures from Proverbs apply to doing Life on Life with our friends?

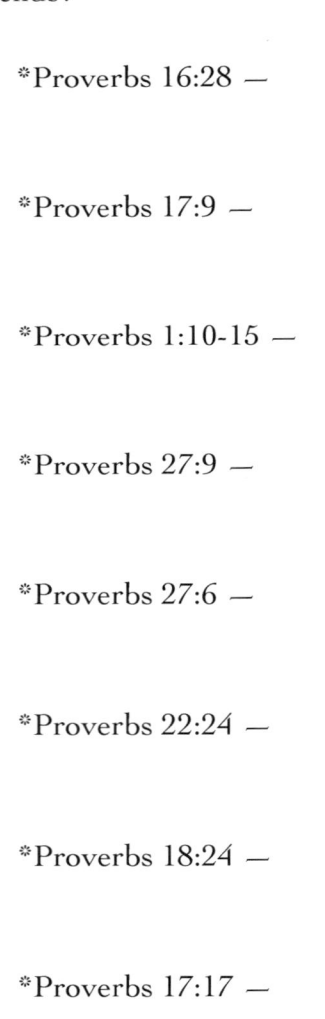

*Proverbs 16:28 —

*Proverbs 17:9 —

*Proverbs 1:10-15 —

*Proverbs 27:9 —

*Proverbs 27:6 —

*Proverbs 22:24 —

*Proverbs 18:24 —

*Proverbs 17:17 —

*Proverbs 12:26 —

*Proverbs 13:20 —

One of the study phrases that we have used is "unpack a passage." Picture unpacking a bag and putting the items away where they belong. As you read the following Scriptures and unpack them, you are putting them away in your heart (your thoughts, beliefs, and desires). As you unpack Scripture about friendship, you will see how important our friendships are intended to be.

*Unpacking Proverbs 27:17 — Please read this in your Bible and note here how it applies to doing Life On Life, One-Another relationships as friends.

*Unpacking 2 Corinthians 6:14 — Please read this in your Bible and note here how it applies to doing Life On Life, One-Another relationships as friends.

*Unpacking Philippians 2:4 — Please read this in your Bible and note here how it applies to doing Life On Life, One-Another relationships as friends.

*Unpacking Romans 12:10 — Please read this in your Bible and note here how it applies to doing Life On Life, One-Another relationships as friends.

Look at your current friendships with other believers, both inside and outside your church. Friendships are challenging because they require selflessness and sacrifice. Are you sacrificial in your approach to your friendships? Do you consider your sister in Christ as more important than yourself? Ask the Lord to reveal what is in your heart towards your friends.

"If you have any encouragement from being united with Christ, if any comfort from his love, if any fellowship with the Spirit, if any tenderness and compassion, then make my joy complete by being like-minded, having the same love, being one in spirit and purpose. Do nothing out of selfish ambition or vain conceit, but in humility consider others better than yourselves. Each of you should look not only to your own interests, but also to the interests of others." (Philippians 2:1-4)

Two women who are coming together as friends both come into the relationship with their own perspectives and expectations. When our perspectives are self-focused or our expectations unreasonable, we can become frustrated with the friendship.

What kinds of perspectives can hinder a friendship? We might misread the friend when we communicate and think that they are saying something that they have not said. We might perceive rejection when they really are just busy that day dealing with their families. We might think that they have a low opinion of us when they really do not. What others kinds of perspectives can hinder a friendship?

How do you gain a proper perspective in friendship? The answer is by now very familiar to you as we study One-Another relationships. It is to APPLY THE GOSPEL. In a friendship, the Gospel is best reflected by forgiveness. We need to walk alongside one another in an attitude of continual forgiveness. We need to let one another "off the hook" regarding meeting our expectations. We need to let ourselves "off the hook" for not measuring up to expectations we think that our friend has towards us. When we offend, we need to seek forgiveness. When we are offended, we need to forgive!

Forgiveness is the most important Gospel reflection in our friendships. Without this Gospel motivated response to one another, there will be no fruit in our attempts to apply the One-Anothers of Scripture in our friendships. Take a few moments now to pray about your friendships, and ask God to reveal to you where you are falling short in being a friend.

"Greater love has no one than this, that he lay down his life for his friends." (John 15:13)

Additional Notes, Lesson Six — Life On Life in Friendship

(Use this for extra homework space and to take notes on our session discussion)

A WORD OF HOPE About Peacemaking

Remember to APPLY THE GOSPEL and THINK BIBLICALLY as you share hope with One-Another.

As long as we are involved in any kind of relationship with one another, there will be conflict. All conflict is the result of sin, as you can see by reading about Adam and Eve in the garden. Adam blamed Eve, and Eve blamed Satan; that is where a poor pattern of handling conflict began and continues today.

The Bible tells us how to make peace with one another. Conflicts between believers are always dishonoring to God. James explains that our conflicts are the result of our evil desires at the core of our heart (refer back to the heart diagram). When we strive to fulfill those desires, we will often fight in order to do so. Instead, we should submit to God.

"What causes fights and quarrels among you? Don't they come from your desires that battle within you? You want something but don't get it. You kill and covet, but you cannot have what you want. You quarrel and fight. You do not have, because you do not ask God." (James 4:1-2)

When we do not handle conflict Biblically, there are consequences. Some of the results of using unbiblical methods of conflict resolution are seeking revenge, verbal attacks, gossip, slander, assault, and lawsuits. Can you think of other results that you have seen in your own relationships? Note them here:

Conflict can be seen either as a struggle or an opportunity. If we remain in the struggle mindset, we are less likely to find victory through the conflict. If we see that conflict brings opportunity to glorify God, to be more like Christ, to serve others, and to bear witness to a watching world, God can be glorified.

There is a difference between peacemaking and peacekeeping.
Peacekeepers want to avoid conflict and will do whatever it takes to do so.
Peacemakers want to resolve conflict and will do whatever God's Word teaches to do so.

When you are helping someone who is dealing with conflict, it is critical that you and they understand the difference between peacekeeping and peacemaking. God calls us to be peacemakers, not peacekeepers. Do you see anything in your own life that indicates that you have been more of a peacekeeper than a peacemaker? Ask the Lord to reveal this to you.

A peacekeeper is a person who struggles with fear, insecurity, people-pleasing, peer pressure, and control, to name a few. These are all under the heading "the fear of man," which we will cover in a future lesson. For now, let's focus on how to be a peacemaker.

"If it is possible, as far as it depends on you, live at peace with everyone." (Romans 12:18)

There are times that peace is out of your reach. You may find that as hard as you try to Biblically resolve conflict, the other person may not be willing to do the same. God does not hold you responsible for the sin of others. If you have done your part, as far as it depends on you, then you have honored the Lord. Peacemaking is a work of the Spirit in our hearts, not something we can muster up on our own. There is great blessing in being a peacemaker!

"Blessed are the peacemakers,
  for they will be called sons of God." (Matthew 5:9)

There are some general peacemaking principles that we have already covered in our study. Let's take a look at how they relate now to peacemaking.
    *Apply the Gospel. A large part of peacemaking is in forgiving the offender, and seeking forgiveness when we have offended.
    *Get the log out of your eye (Matthew 7:3-5). We must take responsibility for our sin in the conflict.
    *Seek forgiveness for whatever fault you have in the conflict, even if it is only a small amount of fault.
    *Extend forgiveness Biblically (see our previous lesson on forgiveness).

The Gospel Is the Key to Peace. A true peacemaker is guided, motivated, and empowered by the gospel — the good news that God has forgiven all our sins and made peace with us through the death and resurrection of his Son (Col. 1:19-20). Through Christ, He has also enabled us to break the habit of escaping from conflict or attacking others, and He has empowered us to become peacemakers who can promote genuine justice and reconciliation (Col. 3:12-14).

✝ A Word of Hope About Peacemaking, CASE STUDY:

A teenage girl in your church youth group, Jessica, has come to you for advice. You have known her for several years because you are friends with her mother. Her mother is thankful for your relationship with Jessica, and appreciates your taking the time to be a mentor to her daughter. Jessica tells you that she and her best friend are fighting. She says they just don't seem to be getting along anymore, and they can't seem to get past the hurts and arguments. They fight about the small things such as which movie to watch when they have a sleepover. They also fight about the bigger things such as how hurt Jessica is now that her friend has a boyfriend and spends more time with him than she does with her. Jessica admits to feeling jealous and hurt. She also admits that she can't find a way to talk to her friend about this, because she is afraid of losing the friendship. She also fears that their other friends will judge her and take her friend's side. She does not want anybody to think she is a bad friend. How would you advise Jessica to be a peacemaker?

Additional Notes, Lesson Six: A Word of Hope About Peacemaking

(Use this for extra homework space and to take notes on our session discussion)

APPLYING HEBREWS 10:25: Fellowship

Hebrews 10:25

"Let us not give up meeting together, as some are in the habit of doing, but let us encourage one another—and all the more as you see the Day approaching."

You will study this most accurately by reading in context in Hebrews 10:19-25, which is the broader passage that this verse is taken from. Remember that our focus for this study is One-Another ministry, so you will want to study that and related themes as you dig in.

Mentor's Bible Study Method Guide

*Meditate *Memorize *Meaning *Meet *Master *Mentor*

Please refer to the Mentor's Bible Study Method Guide in the Introduction for more details on each step if you wish.

<u>Meditate:</u>

Memorize:

Meaning:

Meet:

Master:

Mentor:

BIBLICAL MENTORS: Moses and Joshua

Exodus 24:12

"The LORD said to Moses, 'Come up to me on the mountain and stay here, and I will give you the tablets of stone, with the law and commands I have written for their instruction.'"

You will study this One-Another relationship more accurately by reading about Moses and Joshua in the books of Exodus and Numbers, although the immediate context is in Exodus 24:1-18. In addition to the verses mentioned above, you can understand their relationship more by looking up the other places that their names are mentioned together. Use your Mentor Resource ideas to do this.

Mentor's Bible Study Method Guide

*Meditate *Memorize *Meaning *Meet *Master *Mentor*

Please refer to the Mentor's Bible Study Method Guide in the Introduction for more details on each step.

<u>Meditate:</u>

Memorize:

Meaning:

Meet:

Master:

Mentor:

Lesson Seven

Romans 15:7
"Accept one another, then, just as Christ accepted you, in order to bring praise to God."

LIFE ON LIFE in the Context of Women's Ministry

It is an exciting time to be a woman in the body of Christ. Women are no longer satisfied with the activities of past generations that were typically deemed "Women's Ministry." They now are longing for deeper One-Another relationships with other women, Life On Life. There are more resources now for in-depth Bible studies geared especially for women. There is also a renewed desire for mentoring and discipleship in the spirit of Titus 2:3-5.

In the context of Women's Ministry in our local churches, we have a great opportunity to engage in One-Another ministry. Whether or not your church has a formal mentoring, discipling, or counseling ministry, you can find many places to serve the women in your circle of influence through Women's Ministry.

"I, Paul, am God's slave and Christ's agent for promoting the faith among God's chosen people, getting out the accurate word of God and how to respond rightly to it. My aim is to raise hopes by pointing the way to life without end. This is the life God promised long ago — and He doesn't break promises! And then when the time was ripe, He went public with His truth. I've been entrusted to proclaim this Message by order of our Savior, God himself." (Titus 1:1-3, The Message)

Paul's description of himself in the above passage is a great description for a Biblical Mentor — someone who promotes the faith among God's people, promoting a clear Gospel and teaching others how to apply it. In ministry to other women, it is our responsibility to fulfill that description. Whether we are doing formal ministry or not, we are called to protect Truth by keeping the Gospel message clear and encouraging one another to apply it.

Take a look at your Women's Ministry that you have at your current local church. Are you serving the women of your church in any way? Are you participating in events, either as an attendee or a volunteer? Are you engaged in service projects as they are available? Are you taking advantage of discipleship opportunities, such as Women's Bible Studies and teaching events? Are you participating in fellowship opportunities? Do you pray for or with other women? Do you offer your assistance to the leaders in order to lighten their load and serve them? Take a look now at some ways that you might be able to start to reach women as an encourager who can offer them a Word of hope. Jot down your ideas here:

Serving women requires being present in their lives. Women's Ministries is one context where you can do that by being involved and available. Your Women's Ministry leaders should be interested in your Spiritual growth, and there should be opportunities for that growth to take place. A well-rounded and fruitful Women's Ministry will provide opportunities for women to grow in love, knowledge, and application of God's Word so that they can effectively serve Him in their homes, churches, communities, and workplaces. Bible Studies, Small Groups, Events, Fellowship Activities, Prayer Meetings, Prayer Chains, Meals Ministries (or any service to others), and Outreach Projects are all venues for ministry to one another in the context of Women's Ministries. If these things are not available in your church, perhaps you can pray about whether or not God may be calling you to be the one to implement some change.

Regardless which activities are provided by your Women's Ministry, women will tell you that they are hungry for depth. They are no longer satisfied with "fluff." They long to know God through His Word more deeply, and they long for meaningful fellowship. One excellent way to develop these relationships that include knowing God and His Word more deeply is through mentoring. Mentoring is almost a lost art these days, and it needs to make a comeback. It is not just a nice idea; it is a command in Scripture to "teach the older women to be reverent in the way they live, not to be slanderers or addicted to much wine, but to teach what is good. Then they can train the younger women to love their husbands and children, to be self-controlled and pure, to be busy at home, to be kind, and to be subject to their husbands, so that no one will malign the word of God." (Titus 2: 3-5)

As you engage in Women's Ministry activities, look for women who need encouragement, friendship, discipleship, and mentoring. Make yourself available to them by befriending them, offering to help them, inviting them to fellowship with you, or however God leads you to develop a relationship. By the time you have completed this course, you will have developed discernment and insight in to women and girls, and you will find that the Spirit will lead you to those who need you (and to those that you need, too). If you are qualified as a mentor, it means that you are a woman who is growing in the knowledge of God's Word and how to apply it in your own life first, and then He will direct you to others. If you still feel ill-equipped to mentor others, continue on with this course and take the concepts we are learning to heart. Go back through the previous lessons and read through them again if there are some things you have missed or aren't sure you understand. This is a growing process, and these resources are yours to use from here on. You can also avail yourself to further equipping by taking the next level of Mentor Training if God is leading you in that direction.

Even if you do not see yourself as a mentor, you are still called to do Titus 2:3-5 ministry. There are no additional verses in that passage that let us off the hook in any way. It is for all women!

If you are a woman who wants a mentor, it can be a challenge to find one. The best place to start is to ask! Notice a woman that you are drawn to for some reason — maybe she has skills or knowledge that you would like to learn about, or maybe she has a personality that you are drawn to, or maybe you know her to be a woman with wisdom and counsel to impart. Don't assume that she won't be interested. She may just need for you to ask her! Some generations of women have not been encouraged to mentor, possibly because they have never been mentored. It is time to break this unhealthy approach to Women's Ministry, and it is our responsibility to implement change.

*Older women: it is up to you to become equipped to mentor and to seek out mentees.
*Younger women: it is up to you to seek out mentors and to become equipped to be a mentor yourself.
*Here is a call to the generations:

"One generation will commend your works to another;
 they will tell of your mighty acts.
They will speak of the glorious splendor of your majesty,
 and I will meditate on your wonderful works.
They will tell of the power of your awesome works,
 and I will proclaim your great deeds.
They will celebrate your abundant goodness
 and joyfully sing of your righteousness." (Psalm 145:4-7)

How can you personally become involved in women's lives, especially in the context of Women's Ministry, in order to fulfill your Titus 2 calling? Jot down some ideas here:

Who comes to mind that is in your church family that might be someone who could mentor you? Commit to praying for her and pray about asking her. If there is no one in mind, pray that the Lord would bring someone in to your life.

Who comes to mind that is in your church family that might be someone that you could mentor? Commit to praying for her and pray about offering yourself to serve her.

Commit now to praying for these potential mentors and mentees for the remaining weeks of this course, and let's see what the Lord has in store for your One-Another, Life On Life ministry!

Additional Notes, Lesson Seven — Life On Life in the Context of Women's Ministry

(Use this for extra homework space and to take notes on our session discussion)

A WORD OF HOPE About Fear of Man and Insecurity

Remember to APPLY THE GOSPEL and THINK BIBLICALLY as you share hope with One-Another.

Co-dependency, peer pressure, insecurity, people pleasing, perfectionism and wanting to be the center of attention are all struggles common to women and girls. In Biblical terms, these struggles all fall under the heading "fear of man."

The fear of man is the Biblical term for engaging in any kind of thought process or behavior that indicates that people have become bigger than God in your life. In other words, your relationships with others have more importance in your life than your relationship with God. You may not realize it, because it can be subtle. It can easily become a struggle before you catch it.

The terms listed above are only a few in a list of many that could apply to the fear of man. To give you a better understanding of the fear of man, spend a little time on this introspective exercise.

<u>Some ways that "Fear of Man" may be manifested in your life: check those that apply</u>

*Performance-oriented

*Overcommitted

*Can't say "no"

*Always busy

*Striving to impress and be thanked or noticed

*Perfectionism

*People pleasing

*Afraid of people

*Timid, shy

*Attention-seeking

*Approval-seeking

*Self-promoting

*Elevating people above God

*Overbearing, intrusive

*Feeling like you don't measure up

*Controlled by people

*Controlling

*Easily hurt

*Envy, jealousy

*Easily embarrassed

*Lying, covering up

*Fear of exposure

*Can't make decisions

*Second guessing decisions

*Peer pressure

*Look to people for security, safety, significance, strength

*Concerned with "self esteem"

*Fear of failure

*Doesn't complete (or start) tasks due to fear of failing

*Feeling empty - "love hunger"

*Other people make you angry, depressed, crazy

*Avoiding people

*Feel you are better than others

*Feel others are better than you

*High expectations of others

*Withholding truth, fearing rejection

*Following a crowd

*Gossiping

*Think and feel responsible for other people

*Feel compelled to help people solve their problems even if you don't know how

*Get tired of feeling like you always give to others but no one gives to you

*Blame others

*Feel unappreciated

*Fear rejection

*Feel ashamed of who you are

*Worry whether you are liked or not

*Focus all your energy on other people and problems

*Threaten, bribe, beg

*Saying things that you think will please, provoke, or get what you need

*Manipulate

*Let other people keep hurting you and never say anything

*Feel angry

*Feel like a martyr

*Are extremely responsible OR irresponsible

*Willing to sin to fit in

*Unwilling to seek forgiveness, unwilling to extend forgiveness

*Insecure

*Self righteous

This was by no means an exhaustive list! These are a sampling of some of the ways in which the fear of man manifests itself in our lives. As you identify the things that are manifestations of it in your life, it is important to know that we can assume that everyone struggles with the fear of man in one way or another. It is a universal problem. No one is exempt from it, no matter how mature a believer they are.

Once you have understood fear of man, you can then filter many of your problems through that lens. In a nutshell, the fear of man is being controlled by people instead of being controlled (in the right way) by God.

One example of this would be a teenage girl who tells her mother that she refuses to wear clothing purchased from a discount store because people would judge her and think she is unstylish. The opinions of others are controlling her thinking. These opinions, and therefore, these people are bigger in her mind than God is. Whenever people control us, they are bigger than God in our lives. In One-Another ministry, our challenge is to help others to see that when people are out of proportion in their lives, God is also out of proportion.

The problem isn't the people. The problem is that we want things from people that people are not meant to give to us. For example, we crave honor, respect, approval, affirmation, acceptance, and attention. All of these are a craving for significance. They all indicate that there is a fear of rejection. When we fear rejection by someone, we are controlled by that person. This is the fear of man.

The counter to this common struggle of the fear of man is to have a big God! We need to give God His rightful place in our lives by surrendering to His rightful control over us. When you are controlled by God through His Holy Spirit, then people are brought down to their proper size and place in your life. The solution is not to make ourselves bigger so that people can't control us, but to make God bigger by believing and applying the Gospel, believing His promises, obeying His commands, and following His principles. When we walk closely with the Lord, people's control over us will lessen naturally.

We can apply the Gospel to the fear of man by understanding that the finished work of Christ on the cross tells us that we have been approved, accepted, respected, and we will never be rejected. We possess all of these great benefits in Christ, so why crave them from people? We already have everything we crave in Christ. Jesus is our example of having such a dynamic relationship with God the Father that people never controlled Him. Because of this, He was able to serve others in love. If we need others in unhealthy ways, we cannot serve them in love. Fear of man is a hindrance to One-Another, Life on Life relationships.

The antidote to the fear of man is the fear of God. This is a healthy and proper fear that gives God the respect and honor He is due. The following list is a resource for you to read through when you need the reminder to fear God more than you fear man, and to share with women and girls with whom you are sharing a Word of hope.

According to the Bible, if you fear God you:

1. Walk in His ways, love and serve Him with all of your heart – Deuteronomy 10:12
2. Hate evil, pride, arrogance and the perverted mouth – Proverbs 8:13; Exodus 20:20
3. Are a truly humble person because of your relationship with God – Proverbs 8:13; 15:33
4. Are being honored by the Lord – Proverbs 15:33
5. Obey His commandments – Ecclesiastes 12:13; Psalm 128:1
6. Are being blessed by the Lord – Psalm 128:1
7. Receive wisdom from the Lord – Proverbs 1:7; Proverbs 15:33; Psalm 11:10
8. Are in a frame of mind to receive God's instructions through Scripture in the choices you should make – Psalm 25:12
9. Experience God's goodness – Psalm 31:19
10. Are a special object of God's protection – Psalm 31:20
11. Are truly gracious and generous in a godly way – Psalm 112:4, 15
12. Are a confident, courageous person because of your relationship with God – Psalm 112:6 – 8; Proverbs 14:26; Job 4:6; Psalm 112:7
13. Trust God and are not afraid when evil tidings come because of your relationship with God – Psalm 112:7
14. Are a person who keeps your word, who makes promises and keeps them even if it is to your own disadvantage because of your relationship with God – Psalm 15:4

15. Experience true godly contentment because of your relationship with God – Psalm 112:5, 6, 8, 9; Psalm 34:9

16. Are a godly husband and father (if you are a married man with children) – Psalm 128:1

17. Are a godly wife and mother (if you are a married woman with children) – Proverbs 31:30

18. Receive the benefit of peaceful sleep because of your relationship with God – Proverbs 19:23

19. Are free from an envious spirit because of your relationship with God – Proverbs 23:17

20. Have a solid hope for the future because of your relationship with God – Proverbs 23:17, 18

21. Respect God ordained authorities because of your relationship with God – Proverbs 24:21

22. Avoid intimate associations with people who are disrespectful to God ordained authorities; to people who "are given to change" – Proverbs 24:21, 22

23. Are a place of refuge for other family members because of your relationship with God – Proverbs 14:26

24. Are a source of blessing to other family members because of your relationship with God – Psalm 128:1 – 4; 112:2

25. Are characterized by integrity and faithfulness because of your relationship with God – Job 2:3; 4:6

26. Are truly considerate and kind to other people – Psalm 112:4, 5

27. Persevere in doing what is right because of your relationship with God – Psalm 112:3-5

28. Practice constructive speech in their dealings with people because of your relationship with God – Malachi 3:16; Proverbs 31:30

29. Work hard, but are not so committed to work that you will not have time for enjoyment because of your relationship with God – Psalm 128:3

30. Accept responsibility for your own family and yet are not overly responsible – Psalm 128:1-4

31. Take responsibility for parenting, but not smother and inhibit their children's personal development – Psalm 128:1-4

32. Delight in worshipping God – Revelation 14:7
33. Are free from the fear of man because of your relationship with God – Matthew 10:28; Deuteronomy 1:17; Isaiah 41:10
34. Exercise whatever authority you have in a righteous, God honoring manner without being domineering or authoritarian – 2 Samuel 23:3; Nehemiah 5:15
35. Are willing to submit to the Lord and make sacrifices for Him – 2 Kings 17:36
36. Are a person who praises God – Psalm 22:23, 25; 40:3
37. Know God in an intimate way – Psalm 25:14
38. Stand in awe of God – Psalm 33:8
39. Think much about God's loving kindness – Psalm 33:18
40. Want to encourage others to know God and fear and love and trust Him – Psalm 40:3
41. Receive a godly inheritance of spiritual graces and blessings from the Lord – Psalm 61:5
42. Want to tell others of the great things He has done for you - Psalm 66:16
43. Desire to be with those who fear God - Psalm 119:63
44. Do not want to offend God and you will not take His judgments lightly - Psalm 119:120
45. Have your desires fulfilled; your prayers answered - Psalm 145:19
46. Recognize your own intellectual limitations and be humble about what you know - Proverbs 3:7
47. Recognize that being right with God is more valuable than all of the riches the world may provide - Proverbs 15:16
48. Are zealous in your efforts to try to persuade people to come to Christ - 2 Corinthians 5:11
49. Want to confess your sin and be cleansed of anything in your life that may be displeasing to God; if you are serious about pursuing holiness - 2 Corinthians 7:1, 11
50. Are willing to submit yourself and gladly be in subjection to other believers - Ephesians 5:21
51. Honor other people and have a deep love for other Christians - I Peter 2:17
52. Want to glorify God – Revelation 14:7; 15:4
53. Believe God and His Word – Exodus 14:31
54. Desire with all your heart to magnify the Name of Jesus Christ – Acts 19:17;

Philippians 1:20

55. Receive and respond to the message of salvation in Jesus Christ - Acts 13:16
56. Love to hear and share the message of salvation by grace through faith in Jesus Christ – Acts 13:16 – 43

A Word of Hope About Fear of Man and Insecurity, CASE STUDY:

Shannon is a young adult woman in your church who has come to you to confide in you about some of her relationship problems. She tells you that she has a boyfriend that she has been dating for a year. He also attends your church. She confesses that he has been pressuring her to have sex, even though she has told him that she does not believe it is right. She has had difficulty fighting the temptation and has come close to giving in several times. She is not sure that she wants to keep fighting it, and she is thinking about giving in. She feels that if she doesn't, she will lose the relationship. As you speak with her, you pick up on a common thread in her relationships — she is a people pleaser, a perfectionist who worries about displeasing others, and she fears rejection. Because of these issues with the fear of man, she has made numerous bad decisions in the past. You are concerned that she is about to make another bad decision. How would you share a Word of hope with her? What kinds of things would you say to her?

Additional Notes, Lesson Seven: A Word of Hope About Fear of Man and Insecurity

(Use this for extra homework space and to take notes on our session discussion)

APPLYING ROMANS 15:7: Acceptance

Romans 15:7

"Accept one another, then, just as Christ accepted you, in order to bring praise to God."

You will study this most accurately by reading in context in Romans 15:1-13, which is the broader passage that this verse is taken from. Remember that our focus for this study is One-Another ministry, so you will want to study that and related themes as you dig in.

Mentor's Bible Study Method Guide

*Meditate *Memorize *Meaning *Meet *Master *Mentor*

Please refer to the Mentor's Bible Study Method Guide in the Introduction for more details on each step if you wish.

<u>Meditate:</u>

Memorize:

Meaning:

Meet:

Master:

Mentor:

BIBLICAL MENTORS: Esther and Mordecai

Esther 2:7

"Mordecai had a cousin named Hadassah, whom he had brought up because she had neither father nor mother. This girl, who was also known as Esther, was lovely in form and features, and Mordecai had taken her as his own daughter when her father and mother died."

You will study this One-Another relationship more accurately by reading about Esther and Mordecai in the book of Esther, although the immediate context is the entire chapter of Esther 2. In addition to the verses mentioned above, you can understand their relationship more by looking up the other places that their names are mentioned together. Use your Mentor Resource ideas to do this.

Mentor's Bible Study Method Guide

Meditate *Memorize *Meaning *Meet *Master *Mentor

Please refer to the Mentor's Bible Study Method Guide in the Introduction for more details on each step.

<u>Meditate:</u>

Memorize:

Meaning:

Meet:

Master:

Mentor:

Lesson Eight

1 Peter 4:9
"Offer hospitality to one another without grumbling."

LIFE ON LIFE in the Context of Student Ministries

Whether it's casually meeting for coffee or having an in-depth Bible study, mentors provide necessary spiritual guidance for teenage girls. All girls would benefit from having a godly mentor in their pre-teen and teen years. During these formative years, mentors help girls develop spiritually. This early spiritual growth will help girls stay grounded in college and beyond. With the numerous issues girls face, it is important that they have a godly mentor to help guide and counsel them.

The statistics are shocking — the temptations for teen girls are stronger now more than ever because of the availability and access to those things that entice them to sin. Sexual acting out, drugs and alcohol, and pornography are listed by some teenage girls as their top 3 strongest temptations. With the internet to access pornography, TV shows with explicit sexual scenarios, and common use of drugs and alcohol even on campuses, it is easy to see how girls can fall prey to temptation.

The temptations that girls in our culture face range from what we might call "normal teenage behavior," such as gossip, use of foul language, and lying to their parents, to what we see as more serious things like self-injury, homosexuality, addiction, and promiscuity.

If your heart is not burdened for girls, ask God to break your heart for what breaks His. Titus 2:3-5 mandates the older women to teach (mentor) the younger. We all have a responsibility to the next generation of females, and none of us are exempt from the responsibility. Being a friend/counselor/mentor/discipler/helper of girls is a calling that we all share. How are you currently involved in the lives of teenage girls right now?

If you are not currently involved in the lives of girls, what hinders you from becoming involved?

Mentoring of our youth does not need to be formal or structured. There is a definite need for that type of mentoring, but mentoring of girls can also take place in many more casual, informal ways. For example, girls love to use Facebook and text messaging. Much of your input in to their lives can be done through social networking! If you do not currently use technology like this, consider doing so now. In order to minister to one another, we need to be where "one another" is! Girls are using technology for part of their relationships, and this concept is not likely to go away in our lifetime. If you choose to avoid being where the girls are (including on social networking), you are missing a huge opportunity to minister, Life On Life.

Scripture is full of stories of faithful women who left godly legacies. If Naomi had not mentored Ruth, Ruth would not have followed Naomi's God and become one of His people who was vital to His plan. Young women and girls need your wisdom and godly counsel. They are daily inundated with temptations from our godless culture's telling them to sell out. They are tempted to give away their bodies, minds, and souls for idolatry of self, which only leads to a false sense of self-worth.

It is the older generation's responsibility to reclaim and restore the minds and hearts of our younger sisters in Christ. We do that by engaging in Life On Life, One-Another ministry with them, so that we can offer them a Word of hope. Only God's Word can fill their voids, meet their needs, and change their hearts. Our legacy as Titus 2 women should be to engage in the lives of girls so that they can become rooted in sound doctrine and develop an unshakeable faith so that they are not deceived by every worldly idea or empty promise that is thrown at them.

Did you have mentors when you were a teenager? Who were they, and how did they impact your life?

If you did not have mentors, how do you think your life may have been different if there had been someone to walk alongside you in the spirit of Titus 2:3-5?

One obvious place to get involved with girls is in the context of your local church's Youth Ministry. Your youth pastor or youth director will welcome your volunteer help! He is looking for women to work on his team, because he knows that there is ministry to be done in the lives of girls that he just cannot do himself. Girls need their male pastors as examples of godly men who have dedicated their lives to teaching students to know God's Word and how to apply it. But girls also need women to mentor them, either formally or informally. A well-rounded youth program will have something in place for every student to have an adult who is willing to spend time with them, teach them, encourage them, and admonish them when necessary. Consider whether God is calling you to join your church's student ministry team. They will be thankful to have you join them!

Keep in mind as you work on a Youth Ministry team that your role is not to take the place of a parent. Your team members are partners with the parents, as well as a resource to them. Be very careful not to circumvent a parent's authority in the girl's life.

Many women feel ill-equipped to work with girls. Many others are fearful and insecure about their qualifications. It really need not be as daunting as we imagine the task to be. The following insights are just a few things that girls need to learn from you. You will see that you can, in fact, offer these things to girls regardless of your fears, inadequacies, and concerns.

1. Girls want to know that they are a priority to you. When you set aside time for them, be ready for them. Try not to cancel or be poorly prepared. Girls need to see and hear that they are worth the effort.

2. Girls need your encouragement. Girls are just younger versions of us! We know that they have insecurities and doubts about who they are and what God has in mind for their futures. We also know that they can be self-centered. They need to be heard. Find out what they are struggling with and what they think are their strengths. Find out what their interests are. Ask them about the pressures and stresses they feel as they try to balance school, family, church, and growing up. When you know a girl is struggling, send her a Facebook message or text message to let her know that you care for her and will be praying for her. Share a Word of hope with her at every opportunity. She needs to know that you care.

3. Girls need to know that they can change. Teach her about the heart and how to apply the Gospel. Help girls to discover God's Truths for herself, and guide her as she makes choices and decisions that honor and please God. Support her in any way that you can as she seeks to know God through His Word.

4. Most importantly, girls need to know that Jesus loves them. Remind her often that He does, and that you do, too.

Girls are asking deep questions these days. It is good to be familiar with these kinds of questions, so that when you have a One-Another opportunity with a girl, you are aware of what her mindset might be. Here are a few questions girls are asking:

*How do I know what God's will is for my life?
*How do I know when I am hearing from God and not just making stuff up in my head?
*Why doesn't God seem to answer my prayers?
*What do I talk to God about?
*Why don't I feel close to God?
*If God made me this way, why do I need to change?
*How do I know that I am a good Christian?
*Why do I mess up?
*Does prayer really matter?
*Is Satan real? Can He possess me?
*How can I get close to God?
*Why do bad things happen to people?
*Why did Jesus have to die on a cross?
*Is being gay wrong? What if I can't change the way I feel?
*Is one sin worse than another?
*How do I know for sure that I am saved?
*Why is sex before marriage wrong if everyone's doing it?

There are many other common questions that girls are asking, but this gives you an idea about why it is important to be in God's Word and in prayer as you approach relationships with girls. Girls are insightful and observant, and they will not trust you if you don't exhibit a strong, healthy walk with the Lord yourself. Put your armor on, and reach out to your younger sisters in Christ!

Take a few moments to write a prayer here, asking God to bring to mind a girl in your circle of influence that you can befriend and possibly mentor and disciple. Tell him your fears about it, and also ask Him to help you to be willing.

Additional Notes, Lesson Eight — Life On Life in the Context of Student Ministry

(Use this for extra homework space and to take notes on our session discussion)

A WORD OF HOPE About Decision Making and God's Will

❦

Remember to APPLY THE GOSPEL and THINK BIBLICALLY as you share hope with One-Another.

"After this I looked, and there before me was a door standing open in heaven. And the voice I had first heard speaking to me like a trumpet said, 'Come up here, and I will show you what must take place after this.' At once I was in the Spirit, and there before me was a throne in heaven with someone sitting on it. And the one who sat there had the appearance of jasper and carnelian. A rainbow, resembling an emerald, encircled the throne. Surrounding the throne were twenty-four other thrones, and seated on them were twenty-four elders. They were dressed in white and had crowns of gold on their heads. From the throne came flashes of lightning, rumblings and peals of thunder. Before the throne, seven lamps were blazing. These are the seven spirits of God. Also before the throne there was what looked like a sea of glass, clear as crystal.

In the center, around the throne, were four living creatures, and they were covered with eyes, in front and in back. The first living creature was like a lion, the second was like an ox, the third had a face like a man, the fourth was like a flying eagle. Each of the four living creatures had six wings and was covered with eyes all around, even under his wings. Day and night they never stop saying:

'Holy, holy, holy
is the Lord God Almighty,
Who was, and is, and is to come.'

Whenever the living creatures give glory, honor and thanks to him who sits on the throne and who lives for ever and ever, the twenty-four elders fall down before him who sits on the throne, and worship him who lives for ever and ever. They lay their crowns before the throne and say:

'You are worthy, our Lord and God,
    to receive glory and honor and power,
  for you created all things,
    and by your will they were created
    and have their being.'" (Revelation 4)

What a picture this represents! Whenever we struggle with the concept of God's sovereignty, we would do well to read this passage and realize that we cannot mess with God's sovereign plans. He is on the throne, and He will never slip off of it. Nothing we can do, no poor choice or bad decision we can make will ever remove Him from His throne. This Truth should encourage us and help us in our ability to make godly decisions.

We often struggle to understand how to make decisions because we worry that we don't know what God's will is. As you minister to others, you will find that this topic comes up frequently. A very common reason that people seek counsel is because they are struggling with a decision. The following concepts will help you to help others with their decision making challenges.

God's will can be looked at from three different perspectives:
*God's revealed will (His moral will revealed in the Word of God)
*God's sovereign will (such as events that are outside of human choice)
*God's permissive will (He gives us a free will to choose wisely or unwisely)

Your decisions fall under either His permissive will or His revealed will. Decisions that fall under His revealed will are a matter of obedience. Either there is a command to be followed or a clear principle that cannot be ignored. Decisions that fall under His permissive will are those choices that we can make with wisdom, but that are not spelled out clearly in Scripture.

Some examples of decisions that fall under God's revealed (moral) will are:
*Should I stop fellowshipping with believers?
*Should I commit adultery?
*Should I stop praying?
*Should I forgive my offender?
*List some others:

Some examples of decisions that fall under God's permissive will are:
*Should I look for a new job?
*Should I marry this man?
*Should I change churches?
*Should I volunteer for this ministry?
*List some others:

Biblical decision making starts with a willingness to submit your intentions to God's will and to humbly follow His direction. We get tripped up when we don't know how to figure out exactly what God's will *is* in any given decision we face — especially the bigger, life-changing decisions.

Here is a common road map for Biblical decision making. It is not a formula, but rather a guideline to help you and those you are ministering to as you seek to honor God in your choices.

BIBLICAL DECISION MAKING:

1. Start with prayer! Commit the decision to prayer. As you pray, do so with an attitude of trust and obedience. You can be secure in the knowledge that God knows what is best for you. "'For I know the plans I have for you,' declares the LORD, 'plans to prosper you and not to harm you, plans to give you hope and a future.'" (Jeremiah 29:11)

2. Define which kind of decision it is. Does it fall under God's revealed will? Or does it fall under God's permissive will? It is usually easier to make a decision that falls under God's revealed will, because you will find your clear direction in God's Word. If God has already revealed His will on that decision in Scripture, your response is to obey. The permissive areas still require the application of Biblical principles, but sometimes the direction is harder to discern. "Your Word is a lamp to my feet and a light for my path." (Psalm 119:105)

3. Be prepared to accept and obey God's answer. Your will must be submitted to God's will. When we are humble and submissive, we are in the perfect posture for God to reveal and shed light on our decision. "Trust in the LORD with all your heart and lean not on your own understanding; in all your ways acknowledge Him, and He will make your paths straight." (Proverbs 3:5-6)

4. Exercise your faith. Decision making can take time, and you may need to submit your will many times to God throughout the process. Faith pleases God, so by faith trust Him with confidence that He will reveal His will in His timing. "And without faith it is impossible to please God, because anyone who comes to Him must believe that He exists and that He rewards those who earnestly seek Him." (Hebrews 11:6)

5. Seek concrete direction. Gather your data and find out what the Bible says about the

situation. Gain any practical and personal information that relates to the decision, and write down what you learn.

6. Seek counsel. It is always wise to get spiritual and practical advice from the godly leaders in your life. A pastor, counselor, elder, parent, or another mature believer can give you important insight and help you to remove doubts. They can also confirm your inclinations. The caution here is to be sure you choose people who will offer sound biblical advice and not just say what you want to hear. "Plans fail for lack of counsel, but with many advisors they succeed." (Proverbs 15:22)

7. Make a list. What do you believe God's priorities are in your situation? These are things that are not necessarily important to you, but rather the things that are most important to God in this decision. Will the outcome of the decision draw you closer to God? Will it glorify Him in your life? How will it impact those around you?

8. Add to your list the pros and cons connected with the decision. If you find that something on your list clearly violates the revealed will of God in His Word, you have your answer. If not, then you can now see that you have options to help you to make a responsible decision.

9. List your priorities related to this decision, starting with your spiritual priorities. Ask yourself questions that reveal how your decision relates to these priorities. Will the decision hinder your walk with Christ in any way? Will it strengthen it and provide more opportunities to serve Him? If more than one possible choices will fulfill these priorities, then choose the one which is your strongest desire. Sometimes God gives you a choice. In this case there is no right or wrong decision, but rather the freedom from God to choose, based on your preferences. Both options are within God's will for your life and will lead to the fulfillment of God's purposes for your life. This is His permissive will.

10. Act on your decision. If you have arrived at a decision with the sincere intention of pleasing the heart of God, incorporating biblical principles and wise counsel, you can proceed with confidence knowing that God will work out His purposes through your decision. "And we know that in all things God works for the good of those who love Him, who have been called according to His purpose." (Romans 8:28)

A Word of Hope About Decision Making and God's Will, CASE STUDY:

A 16 year old girl that you are mentoring, Kelsey, is facing two decisions, and she has asked you for some advice. Her first decision is whether or not she should look for a job. Her parents have said that it is fine with them, but they are not requiring her to work if she doesn't want to. She says that she wants a job so that she can start saving to buy her own car. Her dilemma is that she has a very busy schedule already. She has sports after school several days a week, and she is in two clubs on campus that require some weekend commitments. She is active in her church youth group. She is not sure which of her activities she can give up in order to free up the time to work. She is not sure that looking for work is the right thing to do, but she really wants the money. Her other decision that she is facing is related to some peer pressure in her life. Her parents will be gone overnight for one night soon, and her friends want to come over to her house to hang out while they are gone. Her parents have entrusted the house to her, but they haven't given her any specific instructions about whether or not she can have friends over. She knows that the reason they have not given her any instructions is that they trust her and it would not occur to them that she might have friends over without their permission. She has never broken this kind of trust before. Her friends have told her that they won't be doing anything wrong and that all they plan to do is watch a movie. They are trying to convince her that nobody will ever know they have been there. She thinks that maybe they are right, that it would be fun to have them over, and that no harm will be done. She is justifying it because her parents never told her that she couldn't have friends over that evening. She has told her friends to plan to come over. She mentions this to you because she is having second thoughts and wondering if she has done the right thing by telling her friends to come over while her parents are gone. She is worried about making her friends mad, but she is also worried that her parents will find out and be angry. How would you advise her in these decisions?

Additional Notes, Lesson Eight: A Word of Hope About Decision Making and God's Will

(Use this for extra homework space and to take notes on our session discussion)

APPLYING 1 PETER 4:9: Hospitality

1 Peter 4:9

"Offer hospitality to one another without grumbling."

You will study this most accurately by reading it in context in 1 Peter 4:1-11, which is the broader passage that this verse is taken from. Remember that our focus for this study is One-Another ministry, so you will want to study that and related themes as you dig in.

Mentor's Bible Study Method Guide

*Meditate *Memorize *Meaning *Meet *Master *Mentor*

Please refer to the Mentor's Bible Study Method Guide in the Introduction for more details on each step if you wish.

<u>Meditate:</u>

Memorize:

Meaning:

Meet:

Master:

Mentor:

ial Mentors: Elizabeth and Mary

BIBLICAL MENTORS: Elizabeth and Mary

Luke 1:43

"But why am I so favored, that the mother of my Lord should come to me?"

You will study this One-Another relationship more accurately by reading about Elizabeth and Mary in Luke 1:26-56. In addition to the verses mentioned above, you can understand their relationship more by looking up the other places that their names are mentioned together. Use your Mentor Resource ideas to do this.

Mentor's Bible Study Method Guide

*Meditate *Memorize *Meaning *Meet *Master *Mentor*

Please refer to the Mentor's Bible Study Method Guide in the Introduction for more details on each step.

<u>Meditate:</u>

Memorize:

Meaning:

Meet:

Master:

Mentor:

Lesson Nine

Ephesians 4:2
"*Be completely humble and gentle; be patient, bearing with one another in love.*"

LIFE ON LIFE, Ministry with Difficult People

One of the most challenging aspects of One-Another ministry is dealing with difficult people. These are people who need discipleship, friendship, and love, but seem to challenge you at every turn as you try to provide that help. How should you respond and minister in these situations? Everyone has to relate to difficult people — and most of us have been difficult people ourselves at one time or another! Therefore, every Christian should know how to apply the Gospel in these relationships.

"Above all, love each other deeply, because love covers over a multitude of sins." (1 Peter 4:8)

We are called to "love each other deeply." The word translated "deeply" can also mean "constant." "Keep love constant" would be another way to translate that sentence. The word "constant" describes something that is stretched or extended. The love of believers keeps stretching in both depth and endurance. This kind of persevering love can only grow out of the Gospel. You must apply the Gospel to your difficult relationships if you are going to find the strength and endurance to go the distance with people. You must grasp the vastness of Christ's love for you before you can love others with the same kind of love.

"For this reason I kneel before the Father, from whom His whole family in heaven and on earth derives its name. I pray that out of His glorious riches He may strengthen you with power through His Spirit in your inner being, so that Christ may dwell in your hearts through faith. And I pray that you, being rooted and established in love, may have power, together with all the saints, to grasp how wide and long and high and deep is the love of Christ, and to know this love that surpasses knowledge — that you may be filled to the measure of all the fullness of God." (Ephesians 3:14-19)

Do not write down any names, but for a moment, think about those people in your life that are difficult people. What makes them difficult for you? Be honest before the Lord and confess if you have not been motivated by the Gospel towards them by loving them as Christ would have you love them.

There are many types of people that might fall under this heading of "difficult people" in our churches. Sometimes it is just a matter of a personality clash. Sometimes, however, it is more serious than that. Some of these people may exhibit any of the following personality traits:

*Extremely needy people (attention-seeking, intrusive, lack of social skills)
*Unstable or mentally ill people
*People who are unwilling to heed advice
*"Prickly people" who are negative, critical, judgmental and rude
*People who make inappropriate comments during conversation or public discussions
*Arrogant people
*People who lack tact and are too blunt
*People who appear to be always asking but never giving
*People who use other people
*Leaders who lead without grace and love
*Self-focused, self-centered people
*Manipulative or controlling people
*Can you think of others?

God calls us to serve difficult people. He does not make exceptions, although sometimes He does allow for us to set appropriate boundaries with difficult people. We will focus on the concept of boundaries in a future lesson. Our goal in One-Another, Life On Life ministry is to reflect Christ to one another. We imitate Christ by moving *towards* lonely, hurting, wounded, and unlovely people, not by avoiding them. Christ ministered to the outcast, and so must we. The way that we reflect Christ to difficult people is to Biblically love them.

"If I speak in the tongues of men and of angels, but have not love, I am only a resounding gong or a clanging cymbal. If I have the gift of prophecy and can fathom all mysteries and all knowledge, and if I have a faith that can move mountains, but have not love, I am nothing. If I give all I possess to the poor and surrender my body to the flames, but have not love, I gain nothing. Love is patient, love is kind. It does not envy, it does not boast, it is not proud. It is not rude, it is not self-seeking, it is not easily angered, it keeps no record of wrongs. Love does not delight in evil but rejoices with the truth. It always protects, always trusts, always hopes, always perseveres. Love never fails. But where there are prophecies, they will cease; where there are tongues, they will be stilled; where there is knowledge, it will pass away. For we know in part and we prophesy in part, but when perfection comes, the imperfect disappears. When I was a child, I talked like a child, I thought like a child, I reasoned like a child. When I became a man, I put childish ways behind me. Now we see but a poor reflection as in a mirror; then we shall see face to face. Now I know in part; then I shall know fully, even as I am fully known. And now these three remain: faith, hope and love. But the greatest of these is love." (1 Corinthians 13)

1 Corinthians 13 is a Biblical guideline for how to love others. If we unpack it in very simple terms, we can use it as a "checklist" of sorts. Check the way that you love difficult people by looking at what love is according to this passage. Are you patient with the difficult person? Are you kind to them? Are you envious, boastful, or proud towards them? Are you rude or self-seeking? Do you become easily angered towards them? Do you keep a record of wrongs? Are you delighting in the evil that you see, or are you rejoicing with the truth? Are you always protecting? Are you hopeful about this person? Are you persevering with her?

If we are to persevere with a difficult person, we will need to continually address the heart. We need to address our own hearts first; then address the other person's heart.

Yours — God is sovereign, therefore you know that He has ordained that this person be in your life. There are some common temptations to sin that difficult people pose to you. You may be tempted to avoid these people. You may also be tempted to think of yourself as more spiritual and godly than they are. You may try to be too overpowering in their life by trying to change them, or you may try to appease them in order to keep them at a distance. If you are not carefully attending to your own heart, you may sinfully respond to the challenges that this difficult person is bringing into your life. You will be unable to help this person to respond to their life in a godly way when you aren't even responding in a godly way yourself.

Theirs — The more you get to know a difficult person, the more you begin to see the particular types of suffering that person has experienced. You begin to see the way that person tends to respond. You will notice behavior patterns that can reveal much to you about their heart issues (refer back to our heart diagram in earlier lessons). You will realize that you need to be careful not to get sucked in to their emotional states, but instead to focus on the heart issues (thoughts, beliefs, and desires) that are manifesting in their emotions, behaviors, motives, and attitudes. This will help you to see opportunities to help the difficult person to see that their responses are not Biblical. You can then provide guidance during these times, showing them how to apply the Gospel.

In addition to dealing honestly with your own heart towards the difficult person it can also be helpful to keep the following in mind:

*Have Biblical goals as you engage in a difficult One-Another relationship. Sanctification involves back and forth progress. Change happens slowly sometimes and quickly at other times. But change does happen, which keeps you optimistic about the difficult person you are ministering to. Your goal is not to see change at a rate that is comfortable for you, but to remember that God is the One to change hearts, in His timing.

*Redefine love. A great definition of love is found in 1 John 3:16, "This is how we know what love is: Jesus Christ laid down His life for us." Love means death — death to self. Sacrificially loving people is the godliest thing you can ever do. 1 John 3:16 goes on to say, "And we ought to lay down our lives for our brothers." We are not called to "fix" people, we are called to serve them. This is our Biblical priority, which helps us to persevere with someone who does not seem to change quickly. In John 13, when Jesus washes His disciples feet, He gave us a perfect example of persevering servanthood. He did not give up on his disciples because of their imperfections. Some of them could be called "difficult people"! Instead, he served them.

One-Another ministry can be messy. Difficult people need you, and you need them. You need them in the sense that you need to be more like Christ, and your heart towards difficult people often reveals how much you are not like Him. We all need to see how self-centered we can be when we do not redefine love Biblically.

*Apply the Gospel and offer the person hope. Remind them that Christ died to set them free from sin's hold on their hearts, and that in Christ they are a new creation. For some difficult people, change doesn't seem to be very visible or tangible at times. They can become discouraged. One way to offer hope is to help them to set small measurable goals. You can ask them "What do you want to see God do in your life over the next week?" Most people can picture that far in to the future as they imagine living differently over the next few days. Encourage them that change is to be in their heart, not necessarily in their circumstances.

*Encourage the difficult person to serve and love others, too. They are also called to One-Another relationships. Difficult people are often needy people, and the antidote to neediness is servanthood. Help her to find others in her life that she can serve in her family, church, workplace, or social circle. This will help her to see that she is a valuable member of the body of Christ, and that she is not the only person who is struggling. Help her to stay connected to the body of Christ. If she is attending women's Bible studies, small groups, serving in a ministry, and involved in a variety of ways in her local church then she will have many helpers. It is good that you not be her only helper — difficult people need input from several others. It is also beneficial to you that you do not bear the load alone.

*Remember that we are ALL difficult people. Romans 5:8 levels the playing field — "But God demonstrates His own love for us in this: While we were yet sinners, Christ died for us." We may be someone else's difficult person, and we must guard against thinking ourselves better than anybody else. The level playing field metaphor enables us to serve others equally, regardless of their personality difficulties.

Helping difficult people is challenging, but if you see it as an application of the Gospel into the lives of God's people, your love will be more "constant" because it depends less on you and more on the God Who calls you to do it.

Take some time to pray about the relationships that you have with difficult people in your life. Confess to the Lord anything that is hindering the application of the Gospel to these relationships. Ask Him to show you how you can love Biblically, specifically and intentionally. Write your prayer here, and make a commitment to follow God's leading in this relationship.

Additional Notes, Lesson Nine — Life On Life Ministry with Difficult People

(Use this for extra homework space and to take notes on our session discussion)

A WORD OF HOPE About the Thought Life

Remember to APPLY THE GOSPEL and THINK BIBLICALLY as you share hope with One-Another.

"For everything that was written in the past was written to teach us, so that through endurance and the encouragement of the Scriptures we might have hope." (Romans 15:4)

The thought life is the one area that we most commonly struggle with, and therefore we also find it difficult to have hope about controlling it and changing our thought patterns. It is Satan's chief target and the biggest battleground for the enemy's attacks.

As you share hope with others, it is beneficial to ask them about their thought life. This will reveal many things about them, and it will help you to pinpoint what you can say to them to apply the Gospel and to offer hope.

Romans 15:4 reminds us that we do have hope and that His Word helps us to change and gives us the endurance to go through the process of change. The thought life is at the core of the heart, the center of our beings. Out of our thoughts pour our behaviors, motives, attitudes, and emotions. Along with our beliefs and desires, our thought lives must be in line with the Truths of the Gospel if we are to reflect Christ to one another. In order to see how important the thought life is, take another look at our heart diagram on the next page.

HEART CHANGE = VICTORY Ephesians 4:20-24

BEHAVIORS   EMOTIONS/FEELINGS

the mind:
THOUGHTS
BELIEFS
DESIRES

MOTIVES   ATTITUDES

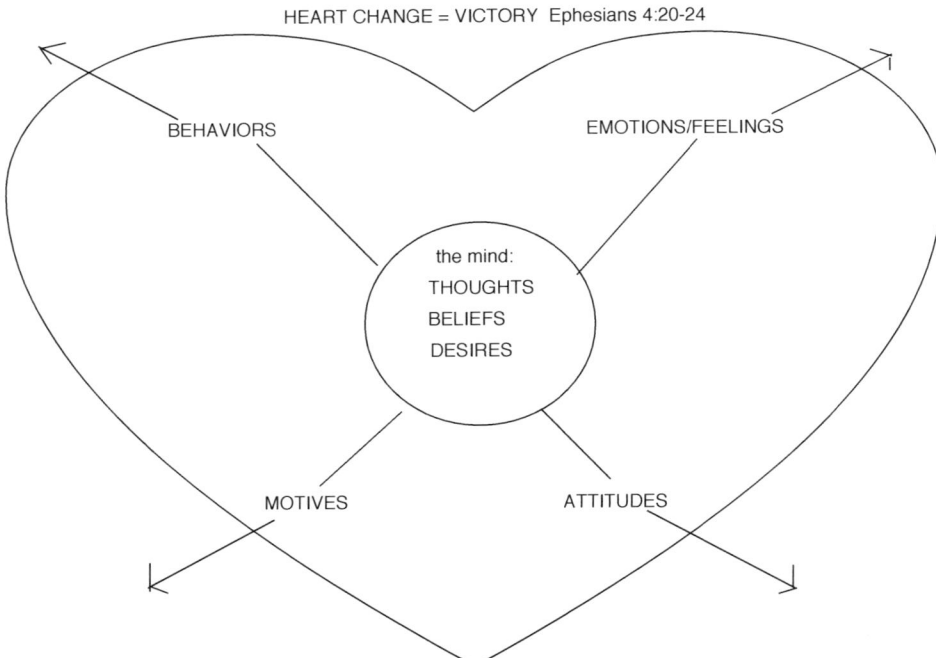

Gospel driven thoughts, beliefs, and desires occur in our minds. They are revealed in our motives, attitudes, behaviors, and emotions, which will flow out of our hearts. Heart change must start by applying the gospel to your thoughts, beliefs, and desires. This will lead to change in your behaviors, emotions, motives, and attitudes. 2 Corinthians 5:17.

There is a principle that we can pull out of Philippians 4:8 that applies well to our thought lives in general. Although this is not the unpacking of a passage in precise context, there is something very applicable in this passage that relates to our thought life in general.

"Finally, brothers, whatever is true, whatever is noble, whatever is right, whatever is pure, whatever is lovely, whatever is admirable—if anything is excellent or praiseworthy—think about such things." (Philippians 4:8)

If we examine a thought through the lens of this verse, we can use the verse as a kind of checklist. For example, we have a thought about our future, such as "I am so worried that someday I might lose my job and not be able to pay my bills, and then I will lose my house." If we look at that thought and examine it according to our Philippians 4:8 checklist, we start with "whatever is true." We have to halt right there, because worrying about something that may or may not happen in the future is not something that is "true"! It may be possible, and we may need to be good stewards about that possibility. However, it is not something we can know for sure, and we certainly should not spend our thought life worrying, which is also distrusting God's sovereignty and care for us. More often than not, we do not get any further than "whatever is true," because many of our thoughts are related to worry, anxiety, and fear.

Another example of how to use this Philippians 4:8 checklist is a thought about something like this — "I am so dissatisfied with my marriage. If only I had a husband like hers. I wish my life could be different and that my husband would treat me the way hers does." Run that through the checklist, and you will see that this thought is true, because it is how she is viewing her marriage. Next on the list is "whatever is noble." The word noble means "high moral principles or ideals." Clearly, you have to halt right here and realize that your thought is not noble. Coveting another woman's husband is not showing "high moral principles or ideals"!

Our thought lives can be controlled. We can have victory over ungodly thoughts, negative thought patterns, hopeless thinking, unbiblical thinking, and bad attitudes. Much of our thought life is spent on things that are not beneficial to our walks with the Lord, and these thoughts develop into a bad habit very quickly. Bad habits can be changed! God has given us the ability to control what we think, and it is up to us with His help and the Spirit empowering us to stop the ungodly thoughts and replace them with new thoughts. We will never be perfect at this until we reach heaven, but we can have victory THROUGH the thought pattern struggles that we all have.

It is helpful to remind one another that Satan cannot enter your mind if you are a believer. He can certainly manipulate circumstances that might cause your mind to think certain thoughts, but he cannot read your mind and cannot inhabit your mind. We cannot blame the enemy for our thought patterns — we need to take responsibility for our own thought lives. If you are engaged in a One-Another relationship with a woman or girl who is struggling with her thought life, you can offer her a Word of hope by helping her to apply the Gospel to her need to control her thoughts as well as apply the Gospel to the particular thought that is preoccupying her mind. For example:

A woman shares with you that she is a believer, but has been feeling very guilty for an abortion that she had 10 years ago. She thinks about this every day, sometimes obsessively. She wonders what the child would be like, and how her life would be different if she had not made that choice. She worries that if she ever tells her family that they will not be able to forgive her. She thinks that maybe God has not forgiven her, because she now understands that she chose to have the life of her baby ended, and she knows this was a sin. You are the first person that she has confessed this to. She admits that these thoughts wake her up during the night, and that the burden has become too much for her to bear. She thinks that she will never be able to stop having these haunting and obsessive thoughts about the abortion.

You listen to her story, and you remind her that when she accepted Christ, she became a new creation in Him, and that He provided everything she needs in His Word for change (2 Timothy 3:16). You remind her that there IS hope for changing her thought patterns (Romans 15:4). Then you gently remind her that if she clearly believes the Gospel, she must realize that her sins are forgiven, including this sin. You may need to go back through the Gospel Story, the Gospel Announcement, and the Gospel Applied (refer back to Lesson One session notes). Recall the diagram below:

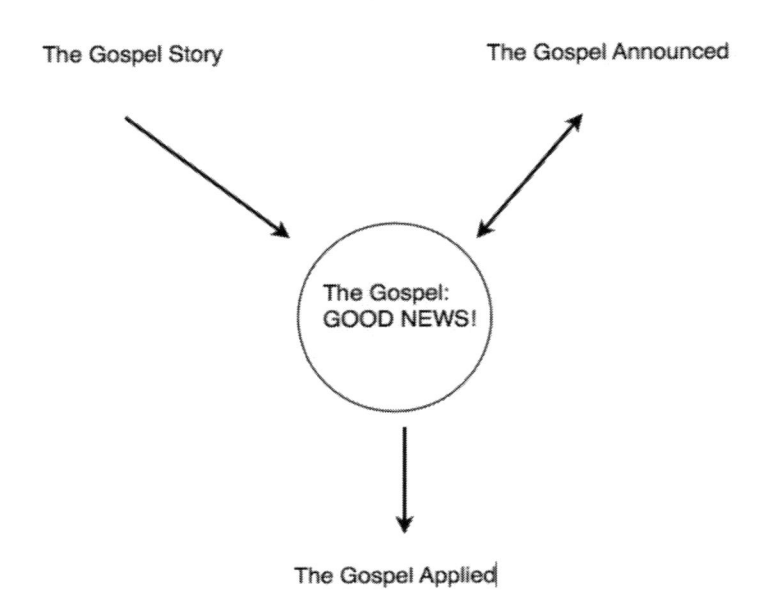

```
The Gospel Story              The Gospel Announced
         \                         /
          \                       /
           ↘                     ↗
            ( The Gospel:
              GOOD NEWS! )
                  |
                  ↓
           The Gospel Applied
```

When she is profoundly impacted by these Gospel Truths, she will know that she is forgiven and she will then be able to start to change her thought patterns. She will need to purposely replace any wrong-thinking with Truth.

There are many ways that you can suggest to someone how to put-off one thought in order to put-on another (Ephesians 4:22-24). For some people, it is helpful to script what they can say to themselves instead of the negative thought. For example, if a person is telling themselves a lie such as "God will never forgive me for that," you can encourage them to stop that thought and instead tell themselves "Jesus Christ paid the penalty for that sin, and God HAS forgiven me." Some people might need to be encouraged to replace the thought by quoting Scriptures that address the thought. Others might be able to stop the thought by listening to theologically sound and edifying praise songs. Sometimes it is helpful to redirect the thought life by getting busy in some other kind of activity to distract the mind from those thoughts. As you walk alongside others, help them to discover what works for them, and offer to hold them accountable to you regarding their thought lives. If you detect an ongoing pattern of thought life struggles that do not change even after you have helped her to apply the Gospel specifically, you will want to consider helping her to find a Biblical counselor who can help her more intensively.

A Word of Hope About the Thought Life, CASE STUDY:

Elizabeth is a 30 year old woman who is married and the mother of 4 children. She goes to your church and you have developed a casual relationship with her as you sit near her in Sunday School. The two of you start talking one Sunday before class, and she admits to you that she is really struggling with some worry about her children. She admits that she has had these worries for years, but has never sought any kind of help for them. You discover that she has intrusive and repetitive thoughts that center around her children's safety. She frequently imagines that her children have serious accidents and that she is not there to protect them. She has even gone so far as to call the school one day to see if her son was all right while she was imagining that he had been hurt in a football game. Even after learning that he was fine, she admits that she was a little surprised when he arrived home unharmed. She realizes that the line between her imagination and reality is getting blurred. She has herself convinced that if she fails to protect her children constantly that harm will definitely come to them. How would you offer Elizabeth a Word of hope regarding her thought life?

Additional Notes, Lesson Nine: A Word of Hope About the Thought Life

(Use this for extra homework space and to take notes on our session discussion)

APPLYING EPHESIANS 4:2: Patience and Forbearance

Ephesians 4:2

"Be completely humble and gentle; be patient, bearing with one another in love."

You will study this most accurately by reading it in context in Ephesians 4:1-16, which is the broader passage that this verse is taken from. Remember that our focus for this study is One-Another ministry, so you will want to study that and related themes as you dig in.

Mentor's Bible Study Method Guide

*Meditate *Memorize *Meaning *Meet *Master *Mentor*

Please refer to the Mentor's Bible Study Method Guide in the Introduction for more details on each step if you wish.

<u>Meditate:</u>

Memorize:

Meaning:

Meet:

Master:

Mentor:

BIBLICAL MENTORS: Paul and Titus

Titus 1:4

"To Titus, my true son in our common faith: Grace and peace from God the Father and Christ Jesus our Savior."

You will study this One-Another relationship more accurately by reading about Paul and Titus in the book of Titus. In addition to the verses mentioned above, you can understand their relationship more by looking up the other places that their names are mentioned together. Use your Mentor Resource ideas to do this.

Mentor's Bible Study Method Guide

Meditate *Memorize *Meaning *Meet *Master *Mentor

Please refer to the Mentor's Bible Study Method Guide in the Introduction for more details on each step.

<u>Meditate:</u>

Memorize:

Meaning:

Meet:

Master:

Mentor:

Lesson Ten

Galatians 6:2
"Carry each other's burdens, and in this way you will fulfill the law of Christ."

LIFE ON LIFE Even While Wounded

One-Another relationships are more than just helping people. They are intentionally building relationships, bearing one another's burdens, and fulfilling the law of Christ (Galatians 6:2). This type of relationship requires honesty and transparency even while (and especially while) we ourselves are wounded. Transparency makes us more human to our sisters in Christ. She sees that we are not any different than she is — we are women just like she is, walking alongside her.

Self-sufficiency is a myth. We all have burdens, and God does not intend for us to carry them by ourselves in isolation from our brothers and sisters. Refusing to allow anyone else to help shoulder your burdens is an issue of pride. It would require an admission of weakness and need. If we avoid admitting that we have burdens, we are denying others the opportunity to apply the One-Anothers of Scripture with us. Those believers who are mentors, disciplers, helpers, counselors, and encouragers are not immune from the very same life struggles that their mentees and students can struggle with.

"I think I am disqualified from ministry." We will be sometimes tempted to make this statement. When we are struggling in our own life at the same time that we are engaged in One-Another ministry with others, family problems, financial setbacks, relationship problems, spiritual strongholds, emotional struggles, and any number of problems that are common to women will also plague mentors, counselors, disciplers, and helpers in the body of Christ. If having problems means that we are disqualified from helping others, then nobody would be helping anybody!

Fruitful ministry is often born out of our own pain and suffering. You are not disqualified because you are in need. In fact, God is allowing suffering and trials in order to equip you for ministry! Of course there may be seasons of struggle in your own life that will require you to step aside from ministering to others in order to find healing yourself. But don't assume that this is always the case. Some of your best One-Another relationships will happen because someone finds you relatable and real. This will require transparency and vulnerability on your part — qualities that all mentors need to develop.

Take some time now to take a look at your own current needs for being ministered to. What areas in your life are you struggling with? What sin issues are involved? What does this struggle reveal about your heart? Write down whatever comes to mind here:

In our lesson about depression, we talked about the purposes of suffering. Suffering in our own lives keeps us relatable in every way to those we are ministering to. The Gospel not only applies to sin issues, it also applies to suffering.

The Gospel does not make you free FROM struggle. It makes you free TO struggle. In our struggles, because of the Gospel, we can be victorious. We are sometimes more concerned about applying the Gospel to an outward sin, such as an addiction, than we are to the suffering that caused that person to become involved in a stronghold in the first place. In our own lives as well as in the lives of our mentees, we must apply the Gospel to suffering as well as sin.

Paul gives us a Gospel-centered perspective on personal suffering in 2 Corinthians.

"To keep me from becoming conceited because of these surpassingly great revelations, there was given me a thorn in my flesh, a messenger of Satan, to torment me. Three times I pleaded with the Lord to take it away from me. But he said to me, "My grace is sufficient for you, for my power is made perfect in weakness." Therefore I will boast all the more gladly about my weaknesses, so that Christ's power may rest on me. That is why, for Christ's sake, I delight in weaknesses, in insults, in hardships, in persecutions, in difficulties. For when I am weak, then I am strong." (2 Corinthians 12:7)

This "thorn in the flesh" is thought to be a physical ailment of some sort, but we can also make application to other forms of suffering. When Christ says "My grace is sufficient for you, for my power is made perfect in weakness," He is helping Paul to apply the Gospel to his suffering. Paul prayed like any of us would pray. He asked God to remove the suffering. Nobody likes personal or physical suffering. However, Paul realized that God had another plan for Paul's life. In that plan, Paul knew that he would be given empowering grace to live it out. This is how Paul applied the Gospel to his suffering. Paul is able to "delight in weaknesses" because he understands the impact that the Gospel has had on his life. He understands that suffering is for God's purposes to be fulfilled in our lives. He also understands that it is because of the power of the Gospel that we can bear suffering and reflect Christ to others as we endure it.

Read 1 Corinthians 1:18-25 and 2 Corinthians 12:1-10. Paul not only understood the Gospel, but he was then able to live it out in a very personal way. The parallel thoughts about the Gospel and personal suffering ("the weakness of God is stronger than men" and "for when I am weak, then I am strong") connect the Gospel to our own personal suffering. The Gospel may appear to be weak to man, but it is stronger than any strength that man can produce. Physical suffering may appear to be weakness to men, but God is able to do more through suffering than man can do through his own optimal strength. A mature Christian, like Paul, not only understands the irony of the Gospel (it seems foolish yet it has power), but is able to bring the Gospel irony to bear on suffering (when we are weak, then we are strong).

Take a moment to do some personal introspection as you apply the Gospel to your own personal suffering:

*What hope do you find in the Gospel as you think about your own current or past suffering?

*How have you found comfort in understanding and applying the Gospel to your suffering?

*Do you believe God's grace is sufficient for you during your time of suffering? Why or why not?

*In what specific ways is God being glorified in your suffering?

We have talked much about applying the Gospel to those who are struggling with sin issues and suffering. Are you in the habit of applying the Gospel in your own life? When we are struggling with sin or suffering, we must hold to what we know to be true about God. We must also worship Him! If we believe the Gospel, then we will also believe that we are called by God to apply the One-Anothers of Scripture. In applying those Scriptures, we will become less intimidated about being transparent in front of one another because we will be more humble while we operate out of a clear understanding of God's grace. The fear of man will not rule in our hearts if we are applying the One-Another passages consistently. The fear of man comes from a self-centered heart. Transparency does not fear man; it reveals Christ in us.

What area of your life have you held back from sharing? What part of your testimony have you been afraid to share, for fear that it will disqualify you from ministry because people might judge you or see you differently? God may be requiring you to become more transparent, not for your benefit, but for the benefit of others.

Thankfully, the success or failure of your One-Another ministry does not depend on your expertise. The emphasis of good ministry is not on the gifts of the minister, but on the power and sufficiency of God's Word. Mentoring, counseling, discipleship, and helping one another are ministries of the Word among ordinary people in everyday life — people like you, who struggle with sin and endure suffering. You are qualified for One-Another ministry! However, if there is something that you are truly struggling with, do not hesitate to get the help that you need. Seek counsel as to whether or not you should step aside from ministry for a season while you get help. Most of the time you will still be able to serve even while you are wounded.

In summary, why do we generally need to continue to minister even while wounded? Because the Gospel applies to our suffering. That is the very message that we need to impart to those in our One-Another circles of influence.

Additional Notes, Lesson Ten — Life On Life Even While Wounded

(Use this for extra homework space and to take notes on our session discussion)

A WORD OF HOPE About How People Change

⁂

Remember to APPLY THE GOSPEL and THINK BIBLICALLY as you share hope with One-Another.

Justification is God's unconditional love for us through Jesus Christ's death on the cross.
Sanctification is the reciprocation of our love toward Jesus.
Glorification is the ultimate reward we will receive when Jesus returns. We will be like Christ.

The Gospel, God's promises, principles in God's Word, and God's commands are all necessary for people to change. Heart change is a result of our salvation. As we approach this subject of how people change, it is good to review the details of salvation.

"For God so loved the world, that He gave His only begotten Son, that whosoever believes in Him should not perish, but have everlasting life." (John 3:16)

Each one of us have broken God's law. This is sin. The wages of sin is eternal death. (Romans 6:23). This price is more than we can possibly repay. Because of God's love for us, He gave his only son Jesus to pay for our debt on the cross. This event is done by Jesus, because He is the only One worthy to pay the price for each one of us since He never sinned. He has not broken God's law like we have. Only He can die a physical death and raise back to life — conquering death! There is absolutely NOTHING we can add to our justification. We are justified by Christ alone.

After justification is sanctification. It's the reciprocation of our love toward God. We are sanctified with the help of the Holy Spirit. Sanctification means to set apart, or to make holy. The Spirit helps us in this process to become like Christ. It is an ongoing life long process. This is not about adding to our justification. That leads to legalism. We are justified in Christ alone, and our love for Him motivates us to live for Him.

Glorification happens after Jesus returns. John writes about this in his first letter when he says "when He shall appear we shall be like Him" (1 John 3:2). Paul refers to our glorification several times. For example: "Listen, I tell you a mystery: We will not all sleep, but we will all be changed— in a flash, in the twinkling of an eye, at the last trumpet. For the trumpet will sound, the dead will be raised imperishable, and we will be changed" (1 Corinthians 15:51-52). He also says, "I consider that our present sufferings are not worth comparing with the glory that will be revealed in us" (Romans 8:18). We get glorified bodies and a new name! We will feast with Jesus, receiving eternal life and being with Him wherever He goes. What HOPE!

Looking at this in the context of applying the Gospel in One-Another relationship, we see that the Gospel provides for our justification upon salvation. The Gospel applied provides for our sanctification. The Gospel makes possible our glorification (when we get to heaven). This is our hope of salvation! As we walk with God in the here and now, we are given the ability to apply the Gospel, follow God's principles, obey God's commands, and cling to God's promises as we are being sanctified.

Sanctification is defined as "being set apart to be holy." Do you view yourself as holy? God views you as holy, because of the Gospel!

"For He chose us in Him before the creation of the world to be holy and blameless in His sight" (Ephesians 1:4).

We need to understand God's view of us before we can undergo Biblical change. Because of the Gospel — Christ's finished work on our behalf — we stand before God blameless and pure. If we are a believer, nothing we do will cause God to view us any differently. We must realize that our motivations to change are not to earn more favor from God or change His view of us. Our motives for change are to love God by believing and obeying His Word, because He loves us and gave His life for us.

The source of all true heart change is: The Gospel.

As you mentor someone who is needing to change because they are not applying the Gospel to their circumstances or to their sin struggles, you will want to first identify the problem. A Biblical mentor or helper of any kind should remember to put the problem in to Biblical terms. We have covered a few of those terms in prior lessons. Another example might be that a girl is wanting to stop habitually shoplifting. She has been labeled by others as a "cleptomaniac." This has become a part of her identity and the way that she sees herself. Biblically, if we are believers, we are not identified by our sin. To identify herself by her sin is to not apply the Gospel to her sin. In Biblical terms, cleptomania is simply "stealing." Stealing is a sin, and therefore there is hope for change!

Once you have identified the problem, you will need to assess their motives. Their motives will reveal whether or not they have clearly understood the Gospel. This will give you a very good starting point. For example, if a woman says that she wants to stop her habit of gossiping, you can ask her why she wants to do that. If she says something like "I want to stop because I don't have any friends left and I am getting lonely," you can acknowledge the validity in that statement, but point out to her that her motive is self-centered and not God-centered. If she says that her motive is "I know it displeases God, and it does not reflect Him well in my life," then you can proceed to help her with the change process, because her motive is God-centered.

Once a problem is identified and a Biblical motive is established for change, you can begin to help her to have hope in her situation. The hope that you share will come from the application of the Gospel and encouragement to follow God's principles, obey God's commands, and believe God's promises.

Biblical change is a work of God (through His Holy Spirit and His Word) in our hearts. In addition to that, there is a part we play in our heart change.

"Do not merely listen to the word, and so deceive yourselves. Do what it says." (James 1:22)

We need to encourage others to "do what it says." We have touched on a great principle found in Ephesians 4:22-24, which we call the "put off/put on principle." When we need to change a particular behavior, we need to follow this principle by identifying what we need to "put off" and also by replacing that with something that we "put on."

"You were taught, with regard to your former way of life, to put off your old self, which is being corrupted by its deceitful desires; to be made new in the attitude of your minds; and to put on the new self, created to be like God in true righteousness and holiness." (Ephesians 4:22-24)

Christians often fail to change, because they try to only change the outward behavior. If you recall our heart diagram, you will remember that behaviors flow out of our thoughts, beliefs, and desires at the core of our hearts. Simply replacing the behavior will not bring lasting change, although it is important to make the appropriate behavioral changes. Replacing our faulty thoughts, beliefs, and desires will bring lasting change. Behavior change will be a natural outcome of heart change. Believers are to put off the old sinful way of life, renew their mind with Biblical Truth, and put on the new godly way of life. Your role is to help them to understand the principle and to walk alongside them while they put it in to practice.

Sinful habits, tendencies, and patterns do not develop over night. They become habits when they are practiced repeatedly over time. Likewise, in order to put off these habits, time will need to be given to practice repeatedly the putting on of the new. We can unlearn unbiblical patterns as we engage in a gradual process that takes place as we put into practice new Biblical principles for living. In time, the old sinful ways will begin to diminish. We are to press on!

"Not that I have already obtained all this, or have already been made perfect, but I press on to take hold of that for which Christ Jesus took hold of me. Brothers, I do not consider myself yet to have taken hold of it. But one thing I do: Forgetting what is behind and straining toward what is ahead, I press on toward the goal to win the prize for which God has called me heavenward in Christ Jesus." (Philippians 3:12-14)

It is helpful to remember that your goal for a mentee is not perfection. Your goal is progress. Perfection will not happen until we are in heaven! Progress should be a part of every believer's sanctification.

In order to know how to guide someone to apply the put off/put on principle, it is vital to have a working knowledge of God's Word. When you don't know for sure what someone should put on, turn to your study resources and do some searching. God's Word does have the answers, but it may take some time on your part to direct someone to them or find them yourself. It will be worth it as you have the amazing privilege of watching God change someone's heart. You get to play a part in that by being an instrument of change as the Spirit uses you to impart Biblical help to one another.

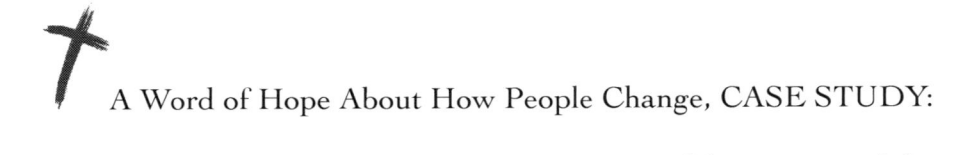

✝ A Word of Hope About How People Change, CASE STUDY:

A casual friend of yours at church, Sandra, confides in you and four other women during a small group discussion at your women's Bible study. She admits that she struggles to stop fantasizing about men that she feels attracted to. She is married to a man who is not a believer, and she wishes that this was different. She has two young children and longs for a godly husband and leader for her family. The subject is not addressed much in the context of this group as women seem uncomfortable with the information. You have a desire to help her, so you approach her individually at a later time and have a private discussion. You learn that her husband is distant and not very attentive, and they have not been having sexual intimacy for the past year. She admits that this is her fault, as she has pulled away from him and he has given up approaching her about it. She says that it is as if they are two strangers living in the same house. She knows that she is not fulfilling her role as a godly wife, and that she has engaged in the fantasizing out of feeling lonely. She admits that it is wrong, and she seems to understand that her desire is to be for her husband alone. She says she has tried to stop, but she just can't. She feels guilty about it, and wants to know how to change so that she can be the wife God has called her to be. How would you encourage and advise her?

Additional Notes, Lesson Ten: A Word of Hope About How People Change

(Use this for extra homework space and to take notes on our session discussion)

# APPLYING GALATIANS 6:2: Bearing Burdens

Galatians 6:2

"Carry each other's burdens, and in this way you will fulfill the law of Christ."

You will study this most accurately by reading it in context in Galatians 6:1-10, which is the broader passage that this verse is taken from. Remember that our focus for this study is One-Another ministry, so you will want to study that and related themes as you dig in.

Mentor's Bible Study Method Guide

Meditate *Memorize *Meaning *Meet *Master *Mentor

Please refer to the Mentor's Bible Study Method Guide in the Introduction for more details on each step if you wish.

<u>Meditate:</u>

Memorize:

Meaning:

Meet:

Master:

Mentor:

BIBLICAL MENTORS: Daniel and Nebuchadnezzar

Daniel 4:34a

"At the end of that time, I, Nebuchadnezzar, raised my eyes toward heaven, and my sanity was restored. Then I praised the Most High; I honored and glorified him who lives forever."

You will study this One-Another relationship more accurately by reading about Daniel and Nebuchadnezzar in Daniel, chapters 1-4. In addition to the verses mentioned above, you can understand their relationship more by looking up the other places that their names are mentioned together. Use your Mentor Resource ideas to do this.

Mentor's Bible Study Method Guide

*Meditate *Memorize *Meaning *Meet *Master *Mentor*

Please refer to the Mentor's Bible Study Method Guide in the Introduction for more details on each step.

<u>Meditate:</u>

Memorize:

Meaning:

Meet:

Master:

Mentor:

Lesson Eleven

1 Thessalonians 5:11
"Therefore encourage one another and build each other up, just as in fact you are doing."

LIFE ON LIFE: Boundaries

As we engage in One-Another relationships, we can sometimes find it difficult to say "no." We can also find it difficult to know when it is time to let the relationship end or change. We may sometimes find ourselves in a position of meaning more to a person than we should, replacing (in a sense) Christ in their lives. We also might tend to think that it is up to us to change a person, as we take on a role in someone's life that we are not meant to fill. All of these scenarios fall under the concept of "boundaries."

Are there "Biblical boundaries"? Or is this simply a psychological term? Boundaries are, in fact, a Biblical concept. We see examples in Scripture of proper Biblical boundaries. For example, God gave a boundary to Adam and Eve in the Garden when He told them, "but you must not eat from the tree of the knowledge of good and evil, for when you eat of it you will surely die" (Genesis 2:17). Essentially, all of His commands in Scripture are boundaries, too. However, when the term "boundaries" is used in the secular psychological realm, it is no longer Biblical. We need to be careful when we use terminology that can be interpreted both Biblically and secularly, making sure that we are using it Biblically and portraying it to others Biblically.

There are different types of boundaries in One-Another ministry. A boundary is an internal "guideline" that lets you know what is and is not your responsibility in the relationship. We have boundaries in many areas of our lives. There are:

*Physical boundaries — have you ever felt uncomfortable when someone is too close to you as they speak with you? We call this our "personal space." Sometimes our personal space is invaded because that person has crossed one of our boundaries.

*Mental boundaries — Your thoughts and opinions are your own. They make you unique and separate from other people. Sometimes we struggle with knowing whether our opinions and beliefs are truly our own, or if we are just imitating someone else's. For example, this is especially true for teenagers as they come to a more adult understanding of faith and needing to make it their own faith, not just because it is the faith of their parents or someone else.

*Emotional boundaries — Emotional boundaries allow you to take in advice or feedback from others without taking in what is not valid. Sometimes we are given criticism that is valid, and we need to act on it. Other times, the criticism is not valid, and we need to be able to deflect it and not effect us.

*Spiritual boundaries — Spiritual boundaries allow you to experience God as He lives in and guides you, but He also allows you free will. God honors your boundaries by giving you the free will to exercise choice.

The secular view of boundaries is a self-centered view. It promotes self-protection and putting yourself and your own needs before others' needs. A believer is called to esteem others more highly than herself and to love others well. There is no room for a believer to be self-centered and self-protective if she wants to have a fruitful One-Another ministry.

Biblical boundaries are Gospel-driven. They require death to self and operating outside of one's own comfort zone. We may be tempted to give up on someone who is difficult because we no longer want to expend the energy the relationship requires. We may feel that the person is intruding on our time, and we feel ready to move on. There may be some other motive for wanting to end the relationship. We need to examine our motives before we can determine what our proper boundaries in the relationship should be.

In order to operate with Biblical boundaries, our motives need to be to love the person well. That has less to do with us and more to do with loving someone as Jesus loves them. We also need to realize that it is God Who sets the agenda in all of our relationships. Recognizing this reminds us that we are all operating within God's sovereignty. If we misuse the word "boundaries," it gives the impression that as a helper we must set boundaries in order to protect ourselves from being taken advantage of. If we think of this in terms of God's setting the agenda, the end result will be that you will love the person well rather than protecting yourself.

As we minister to one another, we may at times need to make appropriate sacrifices. There may be times that it would be appropriate to receive a late night text or phone call, or go to someone's side if they have an urgent need. There are other times that we need to say "no." For example, we may need to tell someone that we are busy but are willing to talk at some other time in the near future. We may need to let someone know that we cannot talk on the phone while we are at work. We need to guard against saying "yes" for fear of being disliked or considered a bad mentor. Saying "no" appropriate at times is an expression of love when done for the proper motives. Extending grace and acceptance of a person does not automatically mean open-ended availability.

It is good to take the initiative to communicate some guidelines for your One-Another relationships and to always let someone know that there will be many times when you will not be available. Be clear about when, how, and where you may be contacted. Doing this with love will prevent many potential misunderstandings later on. Another important reason to set some limits with people is that you do not want it to be too easy for them to go to you instead of crying out to God first. You do not want to be someone who is making it too easy for them to avoid depending upon Christ!

The following boundary check-list will give you some things to consider about your boundaries in your own One-Another relationships. Put a check by any that apply to you:

*I have a very hard time saying "no" to people who seem to need me.

*I feel resentful when someone tells me they need me and asks for my time.

*I tend to over-explain why I am saying "no."

*I feel guilty when I say "no."

*I feel drained by the people I am trying to help.

*I continue to feel obligated to someone even though they have not changed or taken my advice.

A check by any of those on the list indicate that you may not be setting appropriate boundaries in those relationships.

One of the most common boundary issues is knowing when it is time to let go of a mentoring or discipling relationship with someone who does not seem to be changing or growing. If you have spent a fair amount of time applying the One-Anothers of Scripture with this person and you sense that the relationship is not bearing fruit, it is time to examine it more closely.

As a rule of thumb, the fact that someone is not changing is not enough of a reason to give up the relationship. It is God Who changes someone, not us, and we need to let Him do that in His time frame, not ours. In order to discern what to do, we need to look a bit further in to the dynamics of our relationships.

Take some time to unpack 2 Timothy 3:1-5 by reading it in several versions, and then writing down how it applies to the concept of Biblical boundaries. Begin by reading it here in the NIV:

"But mark this: There will be terrible times in the last days. People will be lovers of themselves, lovers of money, boastful, proud, abusive, disobedient to their parents, ungrateful, unholy, without love, unforgiving, slanderous, without self-control, brutal, not lovers of the good, treacherous, rash, conceited, lovers of pleasure rather than lovers of God— having a form of godliness but denying its power. Have nothing to do with them." (2 Timothy 3:1-5)

If you are giving advice to someone and they repeatedly disregard it and show unwillingness to change, it is very reasonable to put an end to the mentoring, counseling, or discipling relationship because they are not willing to submit to the process. Of course you can still be in each other's lives, but the context will change to something more casual. If you are giving advice to someone and they are attempting to put it in to practice (even though they may not exhibit much change), persevere with them because they are showing a submissive attitude and willingness to change.

One good indicator as to whether or not someone is willing to take advice and change is whether or not she is willing to be held accountable. This, too, indicates a submissive attitude towards the One-Another relationship. Any healthy mentoring relationship involves a measure of accountability. Encouraging someone in her walk with God includes encouraging her to be in regular study of God's Word, in regular prayer, and in fellowship. These things are critical to Spiritual health and growth, and we need to have a hands-on approach with those we are ministering to by keeping these concepts as a top priority in our conversations.

People need Christ. They need Him far more than they need you. If you are not careful, you may be tempted to forget that Jesus is the Chief Shepherd, not you. This is a great comfort to a mentor, because it acknowledges that it is Christ Who changes people, not us. We are His instruments for change, but we are not responsible for someone's heart. It is also a comfort to a mentee to know that Jesus is her Shepherd as she relies on Him more than she relies on people.

Those of us in a helper role need to repent of our perceived need to be needed, in control, and successful. These things are idols of our hearts — they indicate that we have not been Gospel-driven in our relationships. We must admit that Jesus is far more concerned and able to help this person than we are. We need to connect people to Christ to remind them as well as ourselves that He is their Shepherd.

Spend some time asking the Lord to reveal to you where you may have some boundary lines that are either being crossed, or that you are crossing in another's life. Write down your thoughts here:

Additional Notes, Lesson Eleven — Life On Life: Boundaries

(Use this for extra homework space and to take notes on our session discussion)

A WORD OF HOPE About Strongholds

Remember to APPLY THE GOSPEL and THINK BIBLICALLY as you share hope with One-Another.

Alcohol, illicit drugs, prescription drugs, eating disorders, pornography, gambling, excessive shopping, excessive exercise, excessive sleep, cigarettes, self-injury, work, sugar, sports, lying, shoplifting, sex, homosexuality, caffeine, television, and internet are all behaviors that we think of when we say "addiction." This is not an exhaustive list. Many other behaviors can become addictive such as seeking status, seeking attention, and seeking approval. Anything that a person craves can become an addiction.

We need to be mindful to put things in Biblical terms rather than psychological terms, as we have covered in previous lessons. You will recall, for example, that we looked at the psychological term depression by using the Biblical terms suffering and despair. We looked at the psychological terms insecurity, co-dependency, and peer pressure by using the Biblical term fear of man. We are now going to look at the psychological term addiction by using the Biblical term spiritual stronghold.

The Bible does not directly use the term "addiction" or "substance abuse." Instead, it speaks of a person's slavery to sin (John 8:34). Scripture also speaks of a person's disposition to evil and depravity that produces sinful passions (Romans 1:18-32). The Bible speaks to idolatry of the heart (Ezekiel 14:1-5).

Addictions are a manifestation of the flesh ruling a person's heart and life, which is idol worship. What we worship become our strongholds.

As you know by now, our goal in One-Another ministry is to apply the Gospel to not only our initial salvation upon belief in Christ's finished work on the cross (justification), but also to our current walk with God as we are being formed in to Christ's image (sanctification), until our salvation is complete in heaven (glorification). In order to apply the Gospel to addiction, we need to first define exactly what an addiction is.

The humanistic psychological approach calls addiction a "disease." Having a disease implies that there is a physiological or biological cause that requires a medical intervention for healing (either physical or psychological intervention). While it is true that of course there is hope in Christ for healing of a disease, most of the time our diseases require some form of treatment. The hope we have tends to depend on the success rate of that treatment. That is a flimsy hope, at best.

If you use the Biblical term for addiction, hope takes on a whole new meaning. An addiction is a spiritual stronghold. Biblical Counselors often use the term "life dominating sin." Scripture has much to say about strongholds, and we will be getting in to that further in this lesson. Applying the Gospel to a spiritual stronghold brings us real hope, not the flimsy hope described above. Because of the Truth of the Gospel, we are free from bondage and no longer prisoners to our sin. We are declared victors, and therefore we can choose holiness over sin whenever we are tempted. We can have victory *through* our struggle with strongholds as well as *from* our struggles with strongholds. This is good news! It is good news that addiction is a sin issue, because if it is sin, then there's hope!

Let's unpack 2 Corinthians 10:4 and see what it says about demolishing strongholds.

"The weapons we fight with are not the weapons of the world. On the contrary, they have divine power to demolish strongholds." (2 Corinthians 10:4)

Keeping this verse in context and reading it along with the broader passage of 2 Corinthians 10:1-5, we see that Paul is addressing the issue of warfare. He points out that although the apostles were living in fleshly bodies, they did not wage the Christian warfare according to fleshly methods or motives. The wordly weapons would include things like swords, guns, and warfare strategy. It would also include wealth, power, influence, or manipulation to accomplish goals.

Instead, a believer uses methods that have "divine power to demolish strongholds." Faith in God, prayer, and obedience to His Word are the effective weapons of warfare for a Christian. These are the warfare weapons that will tear down strongholds. Included in those methods is the application of the Gospel in sharing hope with someone caught up in an addiction, or stronghold.

The things that a person becomes addicted to are things that bring pleasure and a sense of comfort. They become so pleasurable that they are desired more frequently. These things are not sinful in and of themselves, but they can become sinful if they become so important that they grow into idolatry. If someone cannot handle being denied whatever they are drawn to, or if they feel as if they cannot get enough of it, it begins to interfere in their daily lives. They seem to not be able to let go of it regardless of the consequences.

There are usually conflicting emotions as a result of their idolatrous desires. They may say that they feel out of control, stuck, in bondage, and hopeless; and yet, when they indulge their desires they experience an intense pleasure that only feeds further desire. This is where addiction/life dominating sin/strongholds begin. The drive behind it is the desires of the heart.

"And I know that nothing good lives in me, that is, in my sinful nature. I want to do what is right, but I can't. I want to do what is good, but I don't. I don't want to do what is wrong, but I do it anyway." (Romans 7:18-19)

Addictions, or strongholds, are a sin issue. Recall that it is at the core of our hearts where we find our thoughts, beliefs, and desires. When we have sinful desires that we repeatedly indulge, we are quickly caught up in a stronghold. In a One-Another situation with somebody who is in a stronghold, it is important to make sure that they receive the right kind of help. It is very rare for someone with an addiction to a substance or to a sexual sin to simply just "stop." More often than not, they will go through a gradual process of healing, finding victory through the struggle as you walk alongside them and help them to apply the Gospel.

The answers that this person needs are not found in a 12-step program or secular treatment program. The answers are found in God's Word. Depending on the nature of the stronghold, it may be appropriate to refer her to a Biblical Counselor for intensive and long term counseling. A mentor can also play a role in their healing, by holding her accountable and spending time with her as she is healing. In most cases, it will be a longterm process requiring patience, endurance, understanding, and hope.

A Word of Hope About Strongholds, CASE STUDY:

Allison is a woman who recently began attending your church. She has gone to your pastor and admitted to him that she has what she defines as a "drinking problem." She has been a Christian for five years but has not been able to give up her excessive drinking. Your pastor has asked you to come alongside her, to see if you can further assess the severity of her situation and to potentially come alongside her and disciple her. When you first meet with her, she admits that she drinks every evening after work. She typically drinks 6-8 beers or glasses of wine each evening. She says that she becomes jittery and physically very uncomfortable without the evening alcohol. She works as a bank teller during the day and is able to get through the entire day without a drink. As soon as she comes home to her husband and two teenage sons, she craves a drink and begins the daily habit of drinking as she prepares dinner, after dinner, and even more after the family is in bed. She admits that she communicates very little with her sons, as they tend to avoid talking with her. She feels convicted that her drinking behavior is wrong, but she says that she cannot seem to stop. She drinks until she falls asleep, which has hindered intimacy in her marriage. She says that her husband is angry with her and has asked her repeatedly to get help. She has, until now, avoided doing so. She tells you that she is now desperate to stop drinking. She feels that it is ruining her health and her family relationships. She says that she tried to stop drinking cold-turkey about six months ago, but she got some physical symptoms of withdrawal and it scared her, so she began to drink again. What kind of advice would you give Allison? How would you involve yourself in her healing? What kinds of things would you talk about regarding her stronghold of alcohol?

Additional Notes, Lesson Eleven: A Word of Hope About Strongholds

(Use this for extra homework space and to take notes on our session discussion)

APPLYING 1 THESSALONIANS 5:11: Encouragement

1 Thessalonians 5:11

"Therefore encourage one another and build each other up, just as in fact you are doing."

You will study this most accurately by reading it in context in 1 Thessalonians 5:1-11, which is the broader passage that this verse is taken from. Remember that our focus for this study is One-Another ministry, so you will want to study that and related themes as you dig in.

Mentor's Bible Study Method Guide

*Meditate *Memorize *Meaning *Meet *Master *Mentor*

Please refer to the Mentor's Bible Study Method Guide in the Introduction for more details on each step if you wish.

<u>Meditate:</u>

Memorize:

Meaning:

Meet:

Master:

Mentor:

BIBLICAL MENTORS: Samuel and Saul

1 Samuel 10:1

"Then Samuel took a flask of olive oil and poured it on Saul's head and kissed him, saying, "Has not the LORD anointed you ruler over his inheritance?"

You will study this One-Another relationship more accurately by reading about Samuel and Saul in 1 Samuel, chapters 9-15. In addition to the verses mentioned above, you can understand their relationship more by looking up the other places that their names are mentioned together. Use your Mentor Resource ideas to do this.

Mentor's Bible Study Method Guide

*Meditate *Memorize *Meaning *Meet *Master *Mentor*

Please refer to the Mentor's Bible Study Method Guide in the Introduction for more details on each step.

<u>Meditate:</u>

Memorize:

Meaning:

Meet:

Master:

Mentor:

Lesson Twelve

Colossians 3:16

"Let the message of Christ dwell among you richly as you teach and admonish one another with all wisdom through psalms, hymns, and songs from the Spirit, singing to God with gratitude in your hearts."

LIFE ON LIFE in **Your** Life

You have spent the last 12 weeks learning about doing Life On Life with other believers, applying the One-Anothers of Scripture. If you have fully engaged in the homework and teaching sessions, you have gained many Biblical tools that will be useful for your ministry to others in the body of Christ. You are now encouraged to consider how God may be calling you to specifically minister as a mentor to other women and girls.

A Biblical Mentor is a woman who is well equipped to walk alongside other women and girls as a discipler, teacher, and guide. A good definition for a Biblical Mentor is:

"A *follower of Christ who helps* another person reach the important spiritual goal of becoming more like Jesus in every area of their life."

You do not need to have a formal education or a degree or a certification as a counselor in order to help others. There is a place for formal counseling at times. A good Biblical Mentor will know when to refer a woman or girl to counseling. However, much help can be offered through a mentoring relationship. A solid ongoing mentoring relationship may even prevent the need for a woman or girl to have to get more formal counseling. Utilizing the Biblical concepts, principles, and tools you have learned in our lessons will give you the opportunity to help someone grow in their faith. It is a great joy and privilege to serve as a Biblical Mentor as you see God doing a work in someone's heart. It is a ministry of sacrifice as you serve others, and it is rich with rewards as you sense God using you in the life of another.

As you complete this course of study, it is time for you to consider what's next. You were not in this course by accident. God had you in this for His purposes. Those purposes are to be fulfilled in your life according to the Great Commandment (Matthew 22) and the Great Commission (Matthew 28). Before you can discern God's calling on your life as a One-Another minister, it is important to understand the concept of servanthood.

Mentoring others is an important act of servanthood in the body of Christ. Look up the following verses and note what they say about servanthood:

Character qualities of a true servant:

*2 Corinthians 8:9-11 —

*Philippians 4:13 —

*Acts 9:26-30 —

*2 Corinthians 8:8 —

*2 Corinthians 8:1-3 —

*Philippians 2:3-4 —

*2 Timothy 2:14-16 —

Our motives for serving:

*Romans 6:1-11 —

*Romans 12:10 —

*1 Corinthians 15:58 —

*Philippians 2:1-4 —

*Colossions 3:12 —

*1 John 4:11 —

*1 John 5:2-3 —

What should we practice in our service?

*2 Corinthians 4:1,16 —

*Galatians 6:9 —

*Ephesians 6:7 —

*2 Thessalonians 3:13 —

*Hebrews 12:28 —

A quality Biblical Mentor will spend time continually examining her own heart. In Romans 12:1 we are called to be a "living sacrifice." Servanthood is a sacrifice, requiring you to put hands and feet to the Gospel. Ask God to search your heart and to show you anything in your thoughts, beliefs, or desires that are not Gospel-centered and would hinder your One-Another ministry.

"Search me, O God, and know my heart;
test me and know my anxious thoughts.
See if there is any offensive way in me,
and lead me in the way everlasting." (Psalm 139:23-24)

As you continue to consider your personal One-Another ministry, the following lists review and summarize many of the concepts we have covered in our lessons. There is a personal cost to doing any form of ministry. Read through these lists and consider whether or not you are willing to count the cost.

Life On Life, One-Another relationships are:
*Confrontational
*Restorational
*Speaking the Truth in love
*Gospel motivated and Gospel driven
*Two-way
*Transformational
*Transparent and honest
*Vulnerable
*Uncomfortable at times
*Challenging
*Time consuming
*Deeply personal

To be a Biblical Mentor, you should be continually developing the following qualifications:
*Be available
*Be committed
*Be consistent
*Be transparent
*Be a student of God's Word
*Be willing to go out of your comfort zone
*Be gracious

*Be merciful
*Be discerning
*Be selfless and sacrificial
*Be reliable
*Be a listener
*Be practically applying the Gospel in your own personal life
*Be a woman of integrity
*Be a servant
*Be Spirit-led
*Have a mature working knowledge of God's Word

In Luke 14:27-33 (please read it in your Bible), there is a Biblical principle that applies to "counting the cost" of ministry. This passage is about following Jesus, serving Jesus, living for Jesus, and loving God with all our heart, soul, and might. He is to always be first in our lives, and will take second place to no one or nothing. Christians are "cross-bearers." It is in a believer's heart to bear the cross, whatever it may be, whenever Christ requires such. Christ is our Master, and we are called to serve.

To count the cost, we must be profoundly affected by the Gospel. We then realize that God has taken us, wretched sinners, and made us princesses! This costs us the giving up of our former ways and replacing those ways with obedience to God's Word. Consider whether or not you feel that this cost is too high. We have been given heavenly riches in Christ — why would we turn down such an offer? Do you choose to follow Christ, whatever it takes?

Choosing Christ brings great JOY.

"How can we thank God enough for you in return for all the joy we have in the presence of our God because of you? Night and day we pray most earnestly that we may see you again and supply what is lacking in your faith. Now may our God and Father himself and our Lord Jesus clear the way for us to come to you. May the Lord make your love increase and overflow for each other and for everyone else, just as ours does for you. **13** May he strengthen your hearts so that you will be blameless and holy in the presence of our God and Father when our Lord Jesus comes with all his holy ones." (1 Thessalonians 3:9-13)

What has the Lord placed on your heart during the weeks of this course regarding the ministry He has for you? Jot down your thoughts here:

You have worked so hard in this course! Congratulations for making it to the end! God is honored by your desire to grow in love, knowledge, and application of His Word! He has a plan for you and He will lead you to it. Are you willing?

As hard as we have studied, we really have only had a brief overview of our topics. By now you have been introduced to some of the concepts, purposes of, and tools for Biblically mentoring a woman or girl. You have been given a very basic overview of Biblical Counseling concepts as well. You have learned to apply several of the One-Anothers of Scripture as well as looked at some of the examples of Biblical Mentors from Scripture. This overview has equipped you to step out in to some basic mentoring and discipling ministry in the context of your sphere of influence. There is much more equipping to do — we all should be continually challenged to grow in knowledge and application of God's Word.

It would benefit you greatly at this point to take further training if you would like to gain more in depth and specific equipping for Mentoring others. This completed course qualifies you to move on to Level Two of Word of Hope Ministries Biblical Mentor training. Please contact the ministry on our website if you are interested in more details.

www.biblicalmentor.com

God Bless you as you serve Jesus to One-Another!

"May the Lord make love increase and overflow for each other and for everyone else, just as ours does for you." (1 Thessalonians 3:12)

Additional Notes, Lesson Twelve — Life On Life in **Your** Life

(Use this for extra homework space and to take notes on our session discussion)

A WORD OF HOPE About Guilt and Regret

❧

Remember to APPLY THE GOSPEL and THINK BIBLICALLY as you share hope with One-Another.

What does the Gospel say about guilt and shame? We can quickly say the answer to that and this should be the easiest area to apply the Gospel, but it is often where our biggest spiritual weakness is. As quickly as we may answer, we may not entirely believe it as it applies to our own guilt and shame.

GETTING PERSONAL:

The following is a personal testimony by me, Ellen Castillo, the author of this course. This is shared not to bring attention or any credit to myself, but to give glory to God for the way that He has worked in my life. After several years of struggling with my own guilt and shame, He revealed to me where I was not applying the Gospel to my own heart issues. This moment changed my walk with Him in a profound way, and it changed my life forever. I am so grateful. Your story may or may not be similar to mine, but we all have a story to tell. Part of mentoring (or any kind of One-Another ministry) is to share your story with others. I share this story with you now so that I can "mentor" you with it. I have been a type of mentor to you on these pages in every lesson, and it seems appropriate that we get a bit more personal as we close our time together in this course. Sharing personal stories can sometimes be hard, but it always bears fruit. God wastes nothing, and redeems everything. He redeemed my past, and I am so thankful. Here's my story:

Jesus is enough!

I could easily sum up this whole testimony with those 3 words. It is my privilege to share with you something God has done in my life in the past few years.

I once heard a comedienne say that when she was a young girl she had heard Nicky Cruz give his powerful testimony about his life in drugs and gangs, and it was unlike anything she had ever heard before because it was so profound. At that time in her life, she had not experienced much that she thought was worthy of sharing in a testimony.

She then thought to herself "When I grow up, I'm gonna get me a testimony." Then she said, "I did grow up and get a testimony, but it was not the one I wanted."

I could relate to that. As a young girl growing up, life was fairly uneventful and pretty normal. I even remember thinking that bad things only happened to other people. There is not much of a testimony to mention about those years. But then, as an adult in my mid-20's, I did get a testimony, and much of it was not the one I would have wanted either.

After I finished college, I got married and I also began my career working in psychiatric hospitals as an Occupational Therapist.

My entire worldview at that time was rooted in humanistic secular psychology. I was not a Christian at this time, and had the opinion that anyone who claimed any sort of faith was just using it as a "crutch" and not taking control of their own life. I was all about thinking I was in control!

I fully believed that secular psychology held all the answers to life's problems. I think that the whole reason it appealed to me was because it was supposed to make you feel better about yourself, feel more comfortable with life, and just feel good in general. So I was not only all about thinking I was in control – I was also all about being comfortable!

The last thing I would have done back then is look for comfort from the God of All Comfort! I never would have thought that God could fill that void, because I literally did not believe in Him. I even called myself an atheist. I thought that Christianity was, in my wording, stupid. I could never figure out how an intelligent person could believe in something that to me sounded like a fairy tale.

In 1981, we had our first baby. A difficult pregnancy resulted in what I felt at the time was like a nightmare. At two days old, our baby girl died in my arms. I used to believe that when a person died, they just simply ceased to exist. With that lack of hope, I had nothing to get me through the grief but to delve back in to my psychology-thinking that said, "You feel bad, so now you need to find ways to make yourself feel good."

I wanted to be comfortable, so I turned back to my career and psychology and started trying to feel better somehow. I did not feel better, but I was not about to admit that even to myself. Deep down, I had also started to feel really guilty about our baby's death, wondering if an x-ray I had may have caused the genetic disorder she died from. There is no way we could ever prove or disprove that, but that thought was way too painful to face, and I could find nothing in psychology to make me feel better about that feeling of guilt.

So I did what many people do – I shoved it down and refused to think about it. For years I went on like this!

After 7 years of grieving the loss of that baby, some close friends of ours started to have some very obvious changes in their lives. I couldn't help but notice that they had changed, and we started corresponding. I asked my friend Nancy what it was that made her change so drastically, and she saw that as an open door to witness the love of Christ to me. HE is the drastic change that had happened in her life!

Even though at the time I considered it a psychological problem to consider yourself a Christian, I found myself compelled to ask her questions about why she had changed so much. Her answers made me angry at first, and then I would re-read them and start to think maybe she was on to something that I needed.

Then I'd remind myself that being religious was just another symptom of a mental problem, and I'd again think she was just being stupid. Eventually, she did share a very clear gospel message with me, and as a result of those letters, I became a Christian. This was, by the way, to my total shock! But I suddenly completely believed. That was 24 years ago.

Even though I had become a believer, I continued to hang on to much of my belief in secular psychology. I also continued to feel very guilty about our baby's death, and I think I really wanted to even hide it from God somehow.

Remains of my psychology-thinking said "Take care of that one myself, don't give it to God. It's my problem and I will find a way to handle it." I had no idea at the time how seriously that was holding me back as a Christian from truly enjoying God's grace.

On top of the guilt of the baby's death came some more years worth of guilt that I kept shoving down, all as a result of my perceived failures as a mom. As more years past and that mom-guilt (as I call it – you know how they say "guilt" is a mom's middle name) continued to get shoved down, we decided to adopt kids from the foster system.

We had not gotten pregnant for many years, and this was something we had always wanted to do. We added 3 adopted kids to our family within a couple of years, and then as soon as we moved in the final adopted child, I got pregnant. Then two years later, I was pregnant again. Yes, adoption cures infertility sometimes!

By this time, I was a homeschooling mom with 6 kids and had this notion that I was now doing everything right as a Christian mom. We attended a church that reinforced the idea that it was important to "do everything right," so I naively felt that there were some built in guarantees that my kids would be solid in their faith as adults.

Looking back on that era I really think that I believed deep down that my guilt feelings would be cured (or maybe just buried deep enough that they wouldn't keep bothering me) if I just did all the right things. That was my way of trying to take care of it myself — by doing good things to cover it all up. But, that kept coming up empty and I remained plagued by the mom-guilt.

My weak spot is my kids, for sure. If ever I am going to revert to the mom-guilt, it's when my kids are not doing well, even the ones who are now adults. I want to share with you a few things that are part of my current testimony and how God has given me freedom from that mom-guilt in spite of bad circumstances.

Having adopted older and special needs children brings with it some difficulties that I don't think we really fully expected. We had to learn quickly that you don't just love the hurt out of them when a child's past is full of abuse of every kind.

Some of our adult children are not walking with the Lord as I write this. I will leave out any details so as not to betray their privacy. I will summarize it by saying that we have come up against some very difficult and serious things that I never imagined I would have to face as a parent.

So, having alluded to some current very heartbreaking and difficult circumstances with my adult children, am I currently experiencing that mom-guilt again? I can honestly say that, no, I am not (although at times I have been tempted to slip back in to that!)

Because of something that God showed me a few years ago, I have learned that I can trust God in any circumstance. If I begin to revert back to the mom-guilt, it doesn't last long anymore because of what the Lord has taught me through these trials.

I remember several years ago, as I tried to deal with all that mom-guilt that I came to a point of thinking "I accepted God's forgiveness when I got saved, and I believe that He forgives me, so, it must be that **<u>I just need to forgive myself</u>**."

It never occurred to me to first determine whether I was even really guilty! Of course no parent is perfect, but the things that most bothered me and that I felt so guilty about weren't even really things that I was guilty of! But I didn't see it that way then.

I am not sure what it is about moms, but we often tend to take on guilt that is not even ours to carry. If it is our guilt, we can confess, repent, and accept God's forgiveness. If we are feeling guilty about something that we are not guilty of, how silly it is that we would carry that around with us, but we do.

I kept thinking I just need to forgive myself (since I was feeling so guilty). I wanted to do that so that I would feel better about how things turned out with our baby and later with our other kids. I worked at forgiving myself, and worked on it some more, never being able to really forgive myself or understand HOW to do that. I eventually took a particular Bible study that I thought was going to finally teach me HOW to forgive myself, because I was feeling very ready to move on from that.

In the Bible study I took, I read the words "the concept of self-forgiveness is not anywhere to be found in Scripture. It simply is not a Biblical concept."

That was a huge revealing moment. I suddenly realized that I had believed a *lie* that really came right out of secular psychological theory, not out of the Bible. I realized that I had for years tried to do God's job in my life by trying to forgive myself.

I always understood that we are forgiven by Jesus because of the finished work on the cross. I never doubted that, really. I also understood that we are to extend that forgiveness to others. But I threw in this self-centered concept that I also needed to forgive myself.

1 John 1:9 says, "If we confess our sins, he is faithful and just and will forgive us our sins and purify us from all unrighteousness." There is no SELF-forgiveness there – I AM forgiven, my sins were nailed to the cross, and that is enough! If I truly believe that I am forgiven, that takes care of needing to forgive myself!

My children are sinners in need of a Savior, just like you and I. My husband always says that we can't take all the credit for the things our kids do right, so we also can't take all the blame for the things our kids do wrong. Easier said than done for a mom prone to that mom-guilt thing!

I have come to a much better place than wallowing in mom-guilt now. I have HOPE. I have hope, because I know that in my own life Jesus is enough.

I find hope and encouragement in the story of the prodigal son in Luke 15. I know that God would graciously receive my children with open arms if they come to Him, just like the father in the parable.

My job is not to feel guilty about their choices ---- my job is to PRAY.

This self-forgiveness issue was just one of the things in my thinking that was way off base as a Christian, but it was the most important one to get rid of because it literally tripped me up for years. I believe it stunted my growth until God set me free from that line of thinking.

In order to make sure I don't fall back in to that kind of mindset, I have for the past few years been compelled to make sure that I am pressing in to Jesus more than ever before as I enjoy doing in depth study in the Word of God, having a meaty prayer life, and surrendering to a lifestyle of serving God.

I need these disciplines in my life, not because I have to do all the right things anymore – but because I know that on my own, when I am not seeking God faithfully, I am prone to wander. I struggle sometimes with seeking comfort from things other than Christ, even after I realized Christ died to set me free from such behavior. I am prone to avoiding God and trying to take control back in to my own hands. I am prone to spiritual laziness and a weak study and prayer life.

God, in His Word, has SO met all my needs and given me all that comfort and all those answers I was looking for in all the wrong places. Learning to understand and present a clear Gospel, and to apply the Gospel to my heart and life continually has deepened my walk with the Lord and it has also opened many doors for One-Another ministry. As a result of that moment that I realized my thinking about "self-forgiveness" was not Biblical I was launched in to a new lifestyle of ministry as a Biblical Counselor. Sharing a Word of Hope with other women, girls, and their families is something I never would have imagined I would do. As soon as I understood Truth more clearly, I could not hold back and have felt compelled ever since to share that HOPE with others!

Because I've left my former "religion" of secular psychology behind, I have found a new place to look for comfort and for the answers to life's problems. It's called the Bible. The Truth of the Gospel has set me free, praise the Lord!

John 1:1 says, "In the beginning was the Word, and the Word was with God, and the Word was God."

We need add nothing to it!

Jesus IS enough!

✝ This time, YOU are the Case Study. Write down your personal testimony of a time that God helped you to Biblically deal with your own guilt and shame. This can be your salvation testimony, or a testimony of some other time that God did a work in your life that helped you to come to a deeper and clearer understanding of God's grace, mercy, and forgiveness. If you are doing this course in a group setting, please consider sharing a brief version of your story with the group. If you have done this course on your own, you are encouraged to send your testimony to Word Of Hope Ministries (use the contact form on the www.biblicalmentor.com website) if you are willing, so that we can hear how God has worked in your heart.

Additional Notes, Lesson Twelve: A Word of Hope About Guilt and Regret

(Use this for extra homework space and to take notes on our session discussion)

APPLYING COLOSSIANS 3:16: Admonishment

Colossians 3:16

"Let the message of Christ dwell among you richly as you teach and admonish one another with all wisdom through psalms, hymns, and songs from the Spirit, singing to God with gratitude in your hearts."

You will study this most accurately by reading it in context in Colossians 3:1-17, which is the broader passage that this verse is taken from. Remember that our focus for this study is One-Another ministry, so you will want to study that and related themes as you dig in.

Mentor's Bible Study Method Guide

*Meditate *Memorize *Meaning *Meet *Master *Mentor*

Please refer to the Mentor's Bible Study Method Guide in the Introduction for more details on each step if you wish.

<u>Meditate:</u>

Memorize:

Meaning:

Meet: